ULTRA LEADERSHIP

Ultra Leadership

GO BEYOND USUAL AND ORDINARY TO ENGAGE OTHERS AND LEAD REAL CHANGE

Greg Giuliano

AUTHOR OF *THE HERO'S JOURNEY: TOWARD A MORE AUTHENTIC LEADERSHIP*

ULTRA LEADERSHIP

Go Beyond Usual and Ordinary to
Engage Others and Lead Real Change

ISBN   978-1-61961-452-9   *Hardcover*

978-1-61961-444-4   *Paperback*

978-1-61961-445-1   *Ebook*

LIONCREST
PUBLISHING

For Theresa, my ultra wife

Contents

Acknowledgments

IF YOU'RE GOING TO RUN fifty or a hundred miles, you need help. Ultra runners depend upon their crew in order to run the insane distances they do.

The only way I stay on my feet and in the race is with the support of my amazing crew. These generous and talented people make it possible for me to show up and serve our clients day in and day out through the years. Their support and assistance helped bring this book into being.

Thanks to the many runners with whom I've shared some trails and whose grit, determination, and love for what they do inspires me to put on my shoes and get out there.

Thanks to Julie, Kevin, Ian, Adly and the entire publication team for guiding me through the process and helping me make it real.

Thanks to my team, Sina, Bridget, MaryAnn, and the awesome Janet (who has been propping me up since 1989!) for everything you do that makes it all seem easy, uncomplicated, and fun.

Thanks to my colleagues and friends who do the important work of assisting leaders bring about change, especially my partner-in-change, Pat, from whom I learn something new with every interaction.

Thanks to the many leaders who have provided me the privilege and honor to collaborate with them and offer what support I might to their important work.

Thanks to my children, Francesca and Brentano, who make me laugh and whose courage to jump into the world challenges me to be the man they need me to be.

Thanks to my amazing wife and partner, Theresa, who has always seen me as bigger, stronger, smarter, and more capable and courageous than I believed. I am in process of becoming the man she married all those years ago. Our marriage is an ultra; good thing we're there to crew one another. This book is dedicated to her.

Lokah Samastah Sukhino Bhavantu

*"May all beings everywhere be happy and free,
and may the thoughts, words, and actions of my own life
contribute in some way to that happiness and to that
freedom for all."*

Introduction

WE HAVE THREE CHOICES. In every situation, whether we are trying to solve a problem, overcome a challenge, or pursue an opportunity, when things get hard, we always have three options: We can turn back. We can stop in our tracks and spin. Or we can choose to move forward—to push beyond the edge.

I've always believed this. It became existentially real for me one day in 2012. I was running in an ultra marathon event called the TransRockies Run. Over the course of six days, the TransRockies Run spans 125 miles and climbs 25,000 feet. It was day two of the race, and I was making my way up to a spot 12,600 feet up in the Colorado Rockies called Hope Pass. The climb to Hope Pass is a long, taxing part of the race that eventually leads to a majestic view of the Colorado Rockies. It is wonderful when you get there, but that's the problem: getting there.

It was getting there, pushing beyond the edge of what I thought my body was physically capable of doing, that reminded me of a lesson not only about living but about leadership as well. Valuable lessons do not usually come easily, and this one was no different.

I had never done anything like an ultra racing event before. In fact, it was only because my wife, an amazing endurance athlete, was running it that I got involved at all. "Sure," I said. "If you are not concerned about your time, I will do it with you."

The second day of the race climbs up and over Hope Pass on the way to Leadville, Colorado. A race like this was an entirely new physical test for me, and because I had never run or hiked that high before, the experience quickly became an existential one. I was on my way to Hope Pass, climbing switchbacks above the tree line, when Steve Harvey, one of my running mentors, came up to me from behind. Steve is the race director of an ultra running series called Old Goat Trail Races. His nickname is the Old Goat. Don't let the name fool you. He constantly kicks my butt when we run together. On this day, Steve came up on me and asked how I was feeling. Steve, who in 2012 was just shy of seventy, is agile and light on his feet. I was dying just trying to walk up the switchbacks.

"How are you doing, Greg?" Steve asked.

"I'm doing okay," I lied.

"Well," he said, "you've got to keep going because the starting line isn't there anymore. You can't turn back." He gave me a twinkling look and then shot off, running up the trail like a masterful old mountain goat that had climbed these trails hundreds of times.

As for me, I just had to stand there and watch him go. As I continued my climb, I chewed on the notion that my starting line was gone. It was a powerful reminder of what life is about. I could not turn around, because there was no starting line to return to. I couldn't stop, because I was in the middle of nowhere. I had to keep going. It was my only option: to push forward and go beyond my self-defined and self-imposed edge.

As I continued, pushing myself out of my comfort zone and to the edge of my physical ability, I started an inner dialogue. I asked myself, "What do I have control over at this moment?" I knew I couldn't turn back. I knew I couldn't stop. I could only go forward. I had control of my breathing and of taking one step after another. Moving forward was the only thing I could control. *That's what I am going to do,* I told myself. As I was having this conversation with myself, a mantra took shape: *Go to the edge. Push farther. Repeat. Go to the edge. Push farther. Repeat.*

That is how I got to the top of Hope Pass. By the way, Steve was there waiting for me, along with my wife. It was a big, transcendent moment. Tears were shed. Hugs were exchanged. And then my wife said, "Let's go. More trail. It doesn't run itself." And off we went.

MAKING THE CHOICE

Life is a series of choices. So is leadership. In leadership, like in ultra marathons, we must choose to push farther, to move beyond usual and ordinary. I always try to apply life lessons to my work as a coach and consultant for leaders and their teams. I regularly ask myself, *What is my work? What is the lesson here?* The lesson I learned climbing Hope Pass was this: Just as I had chosen to move forward to the edge of my physical ability in the marathon, in the workplace as well we must go to the edge of our competencies and push beyond our comfort zones to achieve extraordinary results.

I began to speak with the leaders and teams I work with about my experience on Hope Pass, what I learned, and what I was applying to business and leadership. The message resonated.

Many leaders tell me that it is becoming more difficult in today's workplace to do their jobs effectively. People are disengaged. Teams lack trust and alignment. Growth is stalled. The way forward is unclear. How, then, do we go beyond usual and ordinary? What does that look like for a leader? What does that look like for a team and organization? Let's push to the edge and embrace the questions, refining and redefining ourselves along the way.

Our inquiry will help us to visualize what it looks like to push beyond the edge, to go farther, grow more, achieve more, and experience more along the way. The work is not quick or easy. It does not happen instantaneously. Leaders must make a conscious decision to work on developing their capacity to lead others. It is a journey on a sometimes challenging trail. Undertaking the journey is how we grow our capacity to lead. It is the decision to go on this journey and build our ability to lead that ultimately distinguishes leaders from those who stop or turn back.

WHO THIS BOOK IS FOR

My hope is that anyone who has the desire to lead, anyone who is curious and interested in learning and growing as a leader, will read this book and use its lessons to take the next step on his or her own leadership journey. The work is never easy, but the journey should be a fantastic experience. After all, there is no turning back. Like the Old Goat told me, "You've got to keep going." The goal of this book is to help leaders take their next steps forward.

But why listen to me? Who am I, after all, to tell you how to lead? What is it about my path that gives me anything to say on leadership?

These are reasonable questions. To get the answer, let's touch on what's been an ongoing debate: Are leaders born or made? Is it nature or nurture? My story is a testament to the view that we can learn to be leaders, if we choose; that it is possible to cultivate the mind-set, skills, and traits required to become a strong and impactful leader; that leadership is, in fact, an intentional choice.

For me, it was almost accidental. I began my career as a high school teacher, and then became a high school administrator. This was very important work, I knew. But it wasn't my important work. So I began exploring my options. While still working as an administrator, I earned a doctorate in psychology. I then went into practice for a few years. Then a colleague introduced me to the field of executive coaching, and I was hooked. Early on I had to leave my comfort zone again when I was called on to lead the US presence of a global consulting organization. From there I went on to found my own firms focusing on change and leadership development. Twenty years later, I have led my own teams, coached hundreds of leaders in various industries at every level, and consulted with teams of every shape and size across the globe. I would never have imagined, right out of college or even when I was working in a high school, that this would be my story. It's been a journey, one in which I have always moved forward by asking, "What's next? What's the next thing to learn? What's the next thing to do? Where can I help?"

I am a firm believer that what happens to us does not have to define us. If we are open to it, life refines us. We all have things that happen to us: some good, some bad. In every situation I've tried to ask, "What can I learn from this experience?" Having a learner's mind-set is a decision to move forward. It is a choice that informs how to live and how to lead. We always have the capacity to reflect on our experiences and to change our reality. Good and bad things happen, but how will you learn from them? Is it a mistake you will never make again? Is it a situation you will never put yourself into again? Is it a rewarding experience that you will strive to understand, harness, repeat, and capitalize on?

Leaders have to make choices, just as I did when I was going up Hope Pass. It's our right to make those decisions—and our responsibility. I could have said, "Oh, poor me.

What am I doing here? I am tired. I am struggling. This is all my wife's fault." But that is a victim's mentality. I chose to be on that trail up to Hope Pass. I chose to put myself in that situation. I had to own my reality.

The same holds true for business. We cannot lead with a victim's mind-set. We have to own our reality. There are no victims in the boardroom. Those there have chosen to be there. They have worked hard to be there, and to play the victim once there is both silly and counterproductive. If I don't like my job or my boss or my career path, I have a choice. If I don't like the results I'm getting or the experience I'm having, I have a choice. What am I going to do about it?

WHAT IS ULTRA LEADERSHIP?

We will discuss what the term "ultra leadership" means in much detail throughout this book, but for now, let's say that ultra leadership means going beyond usual and ordinary. When we talk about leadership, we tend to think about producing business results. That's correct but only partially. Leadership is about pushing the limits, disrupting the status quo, and driving positive change. It is about moving an organization or a project from point *A* to point *B*. It's also about creating high-performing teams to join in that work. And it's about helping individuals develop their capacity to engage and contribute.

That may sound straightforward enough, but it is not a simple thing to do. Leadership is not easy or expedient. Leadership is not a one-and-done enterprise. There's no autopilot. Using a tick-the-box approach will not work. This is what I mean by usual and ordinary leadership. By taking a superficial approach, we fail to generate the alignment, bench strength, and coordinated action required to engage others and drive real change. Engagement remains an afterthought, an HR initiative, rather than a primary responsibility and reflection of an organization's leadership. The usual approach to leadership, the ordinary approach to engaging others and driving change—the phone-it-in, flat, tepid, short-term, power-based approach—is why many organizations suffer from mediocrity.

Mediocre leadership embraces the status quo. It blindly follows rules and polls and procedures. It places too much emphasis on shareholder value. Mediocre leadership places an overreliance on position and power that creates a culture of obedience and compliance. Obedient people only "obey" when the authority figure is watching. Obedient people comply with mediocre leadership. In fact, I hesitate to use the word *leadership* here. Simply put, mediocre leadership, ordinary leadership, does not inspire people to willingly, enthusiastically, and repeatedly engage and contribute. Mediocre leadership relies on coercion or persuasion to drive engagement. Both of these methods have a very limited shelf life.

These shortcomings reinforce why it is so important to change the way we think about leadership. Thinking about this change is where ultra leadership comes in. To most business leaders, change means modifying and improving structures and systems and processes. While that may be true, it does not address the deeper issue of modifying—improving—ourselves.

If we want to lead change, we must change ourselves first. We have to become more conscious and connected and concerned about other people. Then we must push ourselves to the edge of our comfort zones, develop our competence, and raise our confidence as leaders. Pushing beyond usual and ordinary is imperative if we are going to engage others and drive real change.

Doing so requires a fundamental shift in how we think about leadership. We know that leadership is a choice; I think it's time to think of it as a profession. It's a calling. When a superlative engineer or marketer or sales person is promoted into a leadership role, it's important to ask if she has expressed the desire to lead—if she has made the conscious choice to lead—and whether she has the drive to learn and the proper guidance to develop the mind-set and skill set to be the kind of leader the organization needs. Too often, we do not prepare leaders to make that choice and to grow into their roles.

The path of ultra leadership is a lifelong journey of learning and development. It requires a daily decision to lead and a daily decision to learn. We all have our versions of a Hope Pass moment. If we have answered the call to lead, we have to accept what goes with that: an ongoing responsibility to push ourselves to our edges, to learn and grow.

This book provides practical advice and tools for leaders and their teams and organizations. It explores ways in which we can go beyond usual and ordinary and become more conscious, connected, and concerned. We'll examine ways to think more carefully and feel more fully and communicate more effectively in order to create the alignment, bench strength, and coordinated action that enable people to engage and contribute in driving real change.

As we begin, here are some questions to help spark your thinking about ultra leadership.

1. Do you believe that you own your reality?
2. Do you accept that it is leadership, yours included, that determines how strongly people engage and how well they perform?

3. Do you believe that you have the capacity to go beyond usual and ordinary?

4. Are you willing to suspend judgment and consider practicing a new way of leading that goes beyond usual and ordinary?

5. What is something you've done that pushed you "past the limits"?

6. What are you doing right now that is out of your comfort zone?

7. What would "stretching" yourself look like to you and others?

8. What happens if you do nothing, and are you okay with that?

Your answers may be calling you to get back on the trail and move beyond usual and ordinary. I hope so. The more of us who commit to going beyond usual and ordinary, the better. That's how we will engage others. That's how we'll drive real change.

Note to the reader:

Whenever we take in new information, we vote on its value. That's how we are wired. We either make room for the new information and change our thinking and behavior, or we don't. That's fair. My request as you read this book, or any book for that matter, is to slow down that process so that you can carefully consider the possibilities and implications of either accommodating or assimilating new information. That's how we open the door to real learning and development.

CHAPTER ONE

Leadership Today

MOST CHANGE FAILS. Why? Because our capacity to bring change forward is insufficient. Change efforts, especially transformative change efforts, begin with a promise or pledge. Perhaps the promise is that a system in an organization will improve because of change. Or maybe the process that helps generate quarterly growth will surpass previous efforts because of change. Unfortunately, most change efforts fall short of providing a return that is equal to or greater than the investment we must make to affect our desired change. Despite considerable effort and expense, most of our change efforts fail to realize their promise.

A 2013 McKinsey study reported that 70 percent of change efforts fail. The 2013 study was a follow-up to a previous study conducted a few years earlier by John Kotter. In

Kotter's study, the percentage of failed change efforts was also 70 percent. That's a pretty consistent failure rate over time. After years of change management, we're still pretty bad at it.

I see two primary reasons for our persistent inability to lead real and lasting positive change. The first reason is the focus of our change efforts. The focus is usually limited to change management, on process and structure. Successful change requires a focus on leadership before management. Change begins with people; its success depends on people.

The second reason centers on the way we think and make decisions as leaders, and where we direct our efforts in times of change. Only when we widen our focus and strive to think and act more strategically will our capacity for real change leadership grow.

To usher in lasting change, we must begin from the right place. If we start from a place that is not set up to bring forward change successfully, leaders and teams alike increasingly grow disengaged.

Another study, this one conducted by Gallup called *The State of the American Workplace in 2013*, concluded that roughly 70 percent of workers were disengaged. Workers show up; they are at their desks, but they are not as engaged as they could be. They are not willingly, enthusiastically, and repeatedly saying yes when asked to contribute and participate. Internationally, the numbers climbed even higher. Gallup's global study shows that some 84 percent of workers are disengaged. Again, the workers show up, but when it comes to delivering the type of superior work that breaks an organization out of a conventional mold, they fall short.

I've discussed these numbers and the dilemma they represent with leaders across the globe. It seems it's a similar scenario everywhere: people quit, but they stay. They stop working, but they don't leave; they don't pack up their office and go somewhere else. They remain, still collecting paychecks, but for all intents and purposes, they have emotionally and energetically checked out.

In such an underperforming state, without leadership that can drive real change, organizations are trapped in a vicious cycle. It's business as usual. Business moves along. We do more and produce less. We turn unconsciously to outcomes. We keep our focus narrow. We chase short-term wins.

A glaring and harmful characteristic of this vicious cycle is the false sense of urgency that drives most organizations' decisions. It is fascinating to watch leaders talk themselves into believing a task is terribly urgent. Such thinking compels them to think that they must move faster and faster. *Speed up! Do more!* When I hear leaders talk about jam-packed calendars, that everything needs to happen yesterday, that the pace and complexity of their work is a terrific burden, I do not doubt it. I am not trying to diminish the challenges they face. Such busyness is real. But much of it is self-created. For better or worse, everything produces what it is designed to produce. We have designed organizations that don't inspire engagement. We've designed change processes that don't produce real change. In the words of the great Walt Kelly, "We have met the enemy and he is us." Leaders operate under constant pressure, but only some of it is real. The rest is imagined, self-created. Notwithstanding, leaders are asked to accomplish more and more every year, and to do so with fewer resources. How can leaders usher in real change if they are already overburdened, overextended, and shorthanded?

If we look around and see that change efforts are not delivering, that people are disengaged, that leaders are driving toward tactical outcomes and short-term wins, and that organizations are blindly driving ahead, then we begin to see something happening below the surface. Some leaders, when they look at the studies I cited earlier and see the percentages of underperforming workers, say, "Those are problems. We must address those issues." However, the issues are also symptoms. Simply put, the underlying factor in the success rate of engaging our workforce and delivering change is leadership. The underlying common denominator is a failure of leadership that permeates today's workplace.

It is time to reimagine leadership: what it means in theory and what it means in practice, how we choose leaders, how we develop leaders, and what we ask of leaders. We need a new paradigm that distinguishes leadership as a choice, a distinct role, even a profession unto itself. In this new paradigm, it's essential to think about the leadership mind-set and skill set more carefully. It's critical to encourage leaders to embark on an ongoing journey that develops a capacity to lead others effectively, efficiently, and for years to come.

In this new paradigm, the work of real leadership is different than the work of typical, business-as-usual leadership. The work of real leadership—ultra leadership—is to change reality. Consider this: We have a current state, and we have a desired state. Real leadership is about moving an organization or team or project from its current state to its desired state. As a leader, if I move from business as usual to an evolved, dynamic state, I can inspire my team toward higher performance, to progress from point *A* to point *B*. By doing so, I successfully change the reality of my organization.

Leaders drive business results through the work of other people. If I am an individual contributor, I am measured by what I contribute, its merit and impact. If I am a leader, I am measured by my ability to get individual contributors to engage and deliver work. I need contributors to be involved, to provide work of merit and impact. It is a seemingly simple scenario, but it requires the appropriate mind-set and skill set to achieve. As the studies mentioned earlier show, most leaders cannot produce an engaged, contributing workplace. Why?

One reason, as I mentioned in the introduction, is that organizations promote people into a leadership role for which they are not prepared or properly supported. Typically, individual contributors promoted into leadership roles possess a particular mind-set and skill set. Most are subject-matter experts (SMEs)—the engineer, the marketer, the sales person. But that does not always translate into leadership success. Suddenly, a salesperson goes from being a great sales person full of sales knowledge to being a leader without leadership knowledge or the skills to enable leadership success. Now the sales person has to manage a team. Now she has to lead change. The reality is that, in our current paradigm, many people become bosses. Few become leaders. Many times, because those SMEs have not made a conscious decision to lead, they do not cultivate a leadership mind-set and skill set. And, because in most instances leaders retain individual contributor accountabilities in addition to team leadership, they focus on their strengths to stay in their comfort zones. They do not go to the edge of their competence as leaders and push beyond it. They are in default mode, which means continuing to do what they have already been doing. They end up doing much of the work that should be handled by their direct reports because that is also in their comfort zone. If and when some organizations intervene with leadership training, it is in many cases too little too late. Bad habits developed on the fly and over time take hold and are hard to overcome.

How do we know with certainty that a person has the drive to lead? If we do not ask this question, if we just promote the top marketer in the organization into a leadership role and hope he figures out how to lead, we're setting that person up for failure and pretty much ensuring weak and ordinary leadership. It is easy to become overwhelmed and go along with the status quo, to choose the person, at least superficially, who appears best-suited for the job. Doing so is an expedient way to comply and deliver. But, once more, this leads to underperforming people. It takes us backward instead of forward and creates a pattern of disengaged leaders. It's business as usual.

Unprepared leaders lack the skill and drive to step into the challenge of engaging, supporting, and developing a team of people. Unprepared leaders develop work-arounds. The reason they do so is to avoid the hard work of leading people. Heisman winner and Tennessee Titans quarterback Marcus Mariota says, "Sometimes as a leader, you have to...hold people accountable and call them out on things, and that's not an easy thing to do by any stretch." We certainly don't prepare leaders to do this. So they don't. They develop work-arounds. Work-arounds aid the person who has not yet developed the skills to lead properly.

Leadership is not management. Warren Bennis laid out some of the differences in his 1989 book, *On Becoming a Leader*. Leadership requires a unique mind-set and skill set. Success depends on an ability to motivate others to engage, contribute, and deliver. The question becomes: How do I keep my team engaged?

One leader whom I have worked with over the years makes a point of bringing incomplete tasks and strategies to meetings. He invites his staff into a conversation about how, as an organization—not as individuals—they can work together to move toward their goals. The leader defines point B. He says, "This is where we are trying to go." It's a point in the future. He invites the team to examine where they are currently (point A), and to discuss how they will arrive at their desired destination (point B). Simply by being an integral part of that process, the strategy and conversation process, the team becomes much more engaged. Rather than their boss telling them what they need to do, they are asked, "What should we do as a team? What is the best way forward?"

Another example of fruitful engagement-building centers on heightening a team's sense of intrinsic value. When team members understand that a leader cares about them not only for what they produce but also for who they are as people, it goes a long way toward increasing engagement. A team member's willingness to contribute grows because she knows her leader cares about her and the work she does. Engagement becomes a natural occurrence rather than a coerced exercise.

Inviting team members into important business conversations about moving forward, and demonstrating genuine care for individuals, are two simple ways for leaders to inspire engagement. Doing so helps to identify precisely the steps needed for a team to achieve its shared objective. When a leader says, "Here's what we're trying to do. How can we do it?" one team member might say, "In the next quarter, I can deliver A, B, and C." And then another team member might say, "In the next six months, I can produce D, E, and F." When a leader demonstrates a commitment to the team on a person-to-person level and invites team members to own their contributions, engagement levels soar, and team members follow through on commitments.

Think of the coach of a successful sports team. The coach is not on the field with the players. He is on the sideline, teaching and guiding the thoughts and actions of the players. Great coaches come to mind: John Wooden, Phil Jackson, Tara VanDerveer, Alex Ferguson, Billie Moore, Steve Kerr. Great coaches have a unique and distinct role on the team. They try on a regular basis to push players to go beyond their limits and to willingly and enthusiastically and repeatedly give their best, especially over the course of a long season or in challenging game conditions. When players voluntarily show up and give their best despite their own challenges, it is a result of real leadership.

ACKNOWLEDGE THE PROBLEM

We can't fix a problem until we acknowledge it. When we ignore a problem, we exist in it. Disengaged teams stem from disengaged leaders. Disengaged leaders do not want to abandon the status quo. They go after short-term wins and cannot lift their heads high enough to glimpse the future.

I have worked with large organizations trying to implement substantial change, and the level of resistance they encounter can be dramatic. It's not because change does not make sense. It's because some people, leaders included, want to continue to do things the way they have always done them. Rather than address the problem, they switch into survival mode and use the phone-it-in, tick-the-box approach. It's leadership on autopilot.

One example of leadership on autopilot is the performance review. Nobody likes performance reviews. Leaders do not like them, and neither do employees. In theory, a performance review would be used periodically to assess how a person is performing in his or her role in an organization and to help focus that employee's future contribution. But in practice, these reviews have become no more than a structured process devoid of meaning, a ritualized experience that has little bearing on the overall success of an organization.

The manager shows up but wants to end the review as soon as possible because she is so busy and needs to deliver more, faster. The person under review needs to prepare and loses time that could have been spent contributing to a goal. Neither party is eager to have the conversation. It becomes a tick-the-box process.

Moreover, the performance review sets its gaze backward. Leadership is about moving forward, so why are we always looking backward? The performance review is a practice within an organization that has outlived its usefulness unless it is completely rethought. Radical change is required. It's time for leaders to take ownership and forge a new, better way to inspire engagement and maximize individual and team performance. It is time for leaders to go to the edge, to push farther. But what does this mean: to go to the edge?

Peter Andrade is a Senior Vice President at Kaiser Foundation Health Plan. He said, "I was superb as a young leader at processes and fixed sets of management systems. I was good operationally. I had a sincere belief, which was ingrained in me in my first organization, that people did not really matter. People were interchangeable if you had proper processes and systems and numbers management. I believed that for a long time. If you think that way, you do not invest much in people or their development. By age thirty-five, I had mastered that approach. But soon I realized it was not enough. I started to explore how to demonstrate a vision and path to people that would lead them to be more engaged. I learned that having processes and systems is necessary, but if you add to that an interested team that believes in your vision, then performance improves dramatically. I went from being an operationally minded manager to a people leader. That is where I have continued to focus my attention."

Peter's story is appropriate because it succinctly captures what it means to go to the edge, to push beyond usual and ordinary. He made a conscious decision to change. He intentionally explored his possibilities. He dedicated himself to making positive disruptions, all of which led to positive disruptions in his organization, in his team, and in himself.

Peter's transformation touches on how we can change our thinking about leadership. As mentioned, the first step is to acknowledge that what we are doing, the status-quo approach, is not working. As a result, our change efforts fail and our engagement rates are desperately inadequate. We have created a hamster wheel, one that needs to move faster and faster, and it is driving us crazy.

STEP INTO THE VOID

Organizations wanting to reengage people and drive real change must realize that leadership is the determining factor. This book is about rethinking the practice of leadership. What is expected of leadership today? Leadership is expected to engage people to move things forward. How will leaders do that? By adhering to a new leadership paradigm.

The new leadership paradigm is about choosing to lead every day. Every day, in every meeting, in every situation, there is a void. An opportunity exists to step in and lead. I work with a leader who is always looking for the void. This leader is an expert at finding the void and stepping into it. This mentality demonstrates the power of choice: the choice to lead.

Bridget Bisnette is a Senior Director at Cisco. She shared a perfect example of seeing the void and stepping in. "It's easy to lead when everything in the business is going well. The more uncertain the business climate becomes, the more often people sit back, too timid or too afraid to make a mistake or suggest something that may not be embraced by the group. In settings like this the void is palpable, at least if you're looking for it. The void appears when conversations become circular, or when teams are trying to apply the same methods that worked in the past to a new problem.

"In one instance I was in a meeting with fifteen individuals ranging from Sr. Manager to Vice President. The subject was highly complex, and at the time there was no clear leadership on it across the company. I thought, 'Well, that's wrong. There were multiple leaders and they were all headed in different directions.' Therefore, their representatives came to the table with the lens of their leader.

It was noticeable from the start. They even acknowledged it in jest. And, we didn't make any progress. We were approaching the problem from their limited perspective. The opportunity to step into the void and lead came when it was suggested by one person that we reframe the discussion of the opportunity. In that instant the tone changed and the ideas began to flow. It took one person willing to step into the void."

Leadership must see the power of choice in every moment, when it is time to choose between doing business as usual or stepping up to ultra leadership. Be forewarned that stepping up as a leader has consequences. But if success and failure are but parts of the extensive process of change, it is essential to accept them, learn from them, and ultimately continue up the trail toward the greater goal.

One question I regularly ask the leaders whom I coach is, "What's the worst that can happen?" Once I was working with a middle-level executive. He had an idea he wanted to put forth to his superiors but was not sure if it was wise.

"Why would you not do that?" I asked.

"I might get in trouble," he said.

I hit the brakes, fast.

"Hang on a second," I told him. "You're a forty-something-year-old man. Here's a secret: You can't get into trouble anymore. You can get fired. You can get arrested. You can get divorced. You can get injured, but you cannot get in trouble. You're not a kid."

If we are willing to accept the consequences of our actions—successes and failures—then we step forward. We go to the edge and keep going.

There is a legend in ultra running called Caballo Blanco. His given name was Micah True. I came to know about Caballo Blanco through Christopher McDougall's book, *Born to Run*. Each year I participate in an awesome running event in Santa Barbara called the Born to Run Ultra Marathon. The race director is Luis Escobar. Luis was a friend of Micah's. Every year, at the start of each race, Luis asks everybody to raise their hand and swear an oath that originated with Micah True. The oath is the same one that Micah made a small group of folks take as they were about to embark with him on a run through the Copper Canyon in Mexico in 2006. Now every year at Born to Run we raise our hands and say the words, "If I get hurt, lost, or die, it is my own fault. Amen."

There are three choices—in life, in leadership. We must be willing to accept the consequences of trying, of going forward and pushing the limits. We might fail. We might succeed. But either way, no matter what we do as adults and leaders, if we get hurt, or lost, or die, it is our own damn fault. Amen.

Here are some questions to ask yourself right now:

1. Do you find yourself thinking, *If only something or someone would change, then my situation would be better...*, when thinking about your organization, your team, or your life?
2. Do you sit in meetings and think, *What a colossal waste of time!?*
3. Does "business as usual" make your work more challenging?
4. Have you witnessed entrenched corporate culture and bad behaviors kill smart strategies and change initiatives?
5. Are you frustrated at times by your team's performance?
6. Do you find yourself creating work-arounds or saying, "It's just easier if I do this myself"?

Right now, there's an opportunity to step into a void created by an absence of leadership. Will you step in?

CHAPTER TWO

Ultra Leadership

IN 1990, John W. Gardner defined leadership this way: "Leadership is the process of persuasion or example by which an individual or a leadership team induces a group to pursue objectives held by the leader or shared by the leader and his or her followers."

In *Leading Minds: An Anatomy of Leadership*, another Gardner, Howard Gardner, defined leadership as "an individual who significantly affects the thoughts, feelings, and behaviors of a significant number of individuals."

I agree with both definitions, but to my mind a piece is missing. Ultra runners push boundaries by running extreme distances, sometimes as long as thirty, fifty, or one hundred miles or more. Such endeavors go beyond usual and ordinary. Organizations need leaders who, like ultra runners, are not afraid of pushing the limits. We can weave this will to push the limits into our definition of leadership. My simplified definition of *ultra* leadership is this:

The will to push the limits.

The skill to get people to willingly, enthusiastically, and repeatedly engage and contribute to important work.

It's essential to push our limits in all kinds of situations: conversations, meetings, presentations. In each case, ultra leaders move beyond what is expected and deliver rewarding experiences. Doing so takes determination, willpower. The ultra leader does not adhere to the status quo. It's simply not an option, not for an organization, a team, or the leader. Ultra leaders are driven to push the limits, to go, grow, and achieve.

The ultra leader develops the skills to inspire willing engagement that requires no persuasion or coercion. The ultra leader inspires enthusiastic engagement that is energized and passionate about contributing to a stated goal. Ultra leaders, by who they are and how they show up, inspire repeated engagement where people follow their example, step into the void, and look for ways to do more to contribute to the work of driving real change.

THE ULTRA LEADERSHIP FRAMEWORK

My experiences in trail running helped me to crystallize the idea of ultra leadership that I wanted to share with others. I developed the ultra leadership framework over the last couple of years, as my colleagues and I worked with leaders and teams across industries around the world. The goal for us, always, is to grow our clients' ability to lead change and inspire strong engagement and high performance.

The ultra leadership framework illustrates a new way of practicing leadership. It is a beyond usual and ordinary way of leading. The ultra leadership framework provides a way off the hamster wheel. To be an ultra leader is to adopt a new mind-set and develop a new skill set that enables the use of a tool set that reinforces the mind-set and hones the skill set. The ultra leadership framework is made up of elements that, when combined, accelerate one's impact as a leader and produce experiences and results that take a leader and her team beyond usual and ordinary, driving fundamental change and engaging people more effectively.

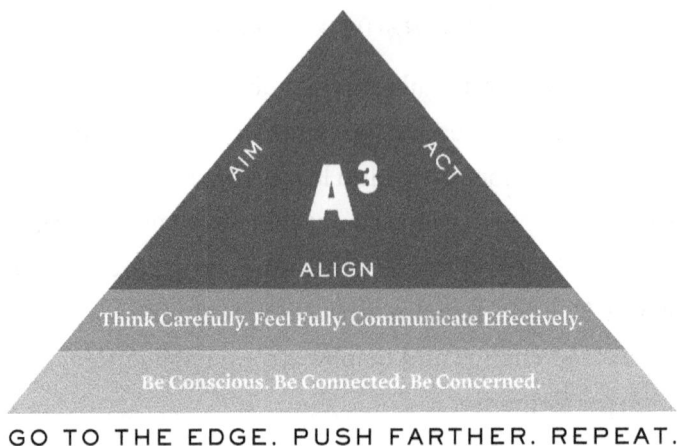

A³

AIM

ACT

ALIGN

Think Carefully. Feel Fully. Communicate Effectively.

Be Conscious. Be Connected. Be Concerned.

GO TO THE EDGE. PUSH FARTHER. REPEAT.

In leadership and life, when we put in the effort to achieve something great, the journey itself is the reward. This is the road Robert Frost describes in his classic poem, "The Road Not Taken." Beginning the leadership journey means growing our self-awareness. In doing so, we must accept not just the positive traits we have accumulated after years of education and experience, but also the shortcomings, the limitations in our selves and in our roles as leaders that hold us back and prevent us from bringing forward successful change. Running exceedingly long distances means accepting that it's going to hurt occasionally. However, if the path were easy, the goal would not be nearly as rewarding in the end. The hard work of powerful leadership development means asking the hard questions.

- What are the things that hold me back?
- What keeps me from fully engaging and impacting people in a positive way?
- What gets in the way of my being the best leader possible?

By asking these questions and seeking greater awareness and consciousness, our capacity to be intentional and impactful leaders grows. I've met and worked with many brilliant and dedicated learning and development professionals over the years. Their contributions to the field cannot be underestimated or overappreciated. They deserve our respect and gratitude. It's important to make clear that traditional leadership development—the philosophies and tactics that for decades have been used to grow and mature organizations—has produced some very positive results and made the workplace better for many. But like anything that we use over and over again, the process eventually grows stale, and the results dwindle. We know this is true from the many studies that indicate leadership and employee engagement reside at perilously low rates. The focus on competency training over personal development—true mental development—means that in many cases people are trained in a technique or tool but lack the cognitive and emotional capacity to know how, if, and when to best use that particular technique or tool.

A new leadership paradigm requires fresh leadership development. A new mind-set and skill set demands that we expand our leadership development perspective. Developing and supporting ultra leadership requires the type of multidimensional development that encourages personal, cognitive, and emotional growth in order to provide the context and foundation for improved competency.

John F. Kennedy said, "Leadership and learning are indispensable to each other." When we push the limits, we learn. We begin to live and lead from a creative rather than a reactive viewpoint.

WHAT AN ULTRA LEADER LOOKS LIKE

Those who choose the path of ultra leadership possess six key attributes.

1. Ultra leaders choose to be present. We need to engage others in the here and now, in the field of shared experience.
2. Ultra leaders choose to be observant. We have to pay attention to what is occurring within our areas of experience. Being observant means taking the time to fully assess and analyze situations before jumping into action.
3. Ultra leaders choose to be creative. Creativity and curiosity go hand in hand. We have to give the time and space to find optimal solutions and not just the obvious ones.

4. Ultra leaders choose to be innovative. We have to consider carefully the advantages and disadvantages of every course of action available before jumping into action. This is when possibilities multiply, and options we have not thought of or experienced before emerge and present multiple paths toward the best possible future.

5. Ultra leaders choose to be strategic. We have to make decisions based on our vision, our mission and values, and put all the pieces together to ensure intelligent action steps.

6. Ultra leaders choose to be purposeful. We come to better decisions about what to do and what not to do and engage people in tasks more purposefully, with more intention.

Ultra leadership begins with this mind-set: Be conscious. Be connected. Be concerned. Of these, I believe that personal consciousness that grows as the result of our ongoing self-reflection, self-discovery, and self-development is the key to becoming an ultra leader. We'll explore what it means to be more conscious, connected, and concerned in the next chapter.

A leader must develop competence at many things. Three skills are foundational to the rest, and we will explore those in depth in chapters 4, 5, and 6. They are the abilities to think carefully, to feel fully, and to communicate effectively.

Careful thinking can be summarized as the capacity to find meaning in confusion, to think strategically, and to generate new and creative opportunities to address challenges. Careful thinking involves being able to encounter confusion, to hold multiple pieces of information in memory at any given time, and to analyze each piece and understand the relationship among the data points in order to lessen confusion.

To feel fully means to be emotionally self-aware and capable of managing emotions and energy to positively engage and interact with others. Feeling fully is about emotional intelligence and resilience.

Communicating effectively involves designing, convening, and engaging in conversations that are vital to connecting with others, driving business, and achieving success. To communicate effectively, leaders must have a capacity for conversing, listening, and clearly presenting ideas to their team members, their stakeholders, and their customers.

The ultra leadership framework includes a model and tool kit (the A^3 model) that reminds us to think more carefully, feel more fully, and communicate more effectively. When we follow A^3, we create shared clarity and alignment, we help those around us grow, we build our team's bench strength, and we ensure that the actions that our team is taking are well coordinated. We will look more closely at the A³ model and the ultra leadership tool kit in chapter 7.

OBSTACLES ON THE PATH

Leaders who start to develop the ultra leadership mind-set and practice its skill set will begin to embody the attributes mentioned above in their day-to-day experience, igniting the spark that is needed to inspire higher engagement and support more impactful contributions. But this mode of leadership—breaking past the usual and ordinary—also presents numerous challenges. Some are external, like rocks and roots on the trail. Some are internal: these are the voices in our heads that lie by saying that we are tired and should stop or that we aren't good enough or smart enough. We need to be aware of these challenges as we set out for every run or every meeting.

One external challenge is the pressure to conform to an organization's culture—to blindly move along, to accept "business as usual" as one's default mentality. The pressure to conform is a powerful external challenge. When leaders attempt to go beyond usual and ordinary, an organization's culture tries to put them back in line. Only when we consciously intend to live the ultra leadership attributes is a new opportunity, or a different path, revealed.

A second external challenge is the need for speed. Organizations today are moving faster and faster, but at what cost? Because our competitors are moving faster, so must we. Part of this pressure is real—contemporary markets do move faster. But part of it is imagined. It is a false sense of urgency that dictates the action of our days. Most often, it is counterproductive, and it stands in our way of becoming an ultra leader. We need to be aware of this pressure, the need for speed. As we prepare to take a step on the path toward ultra leadership, it is important to recognize that our organization might not be amenable to it. We need to know this as we begin our process. The pressure to conform and the need for speed work against us as we try to change how we show up as leaders.

In addition to external challenges, we have internal challenges. Most often, we create these challenges on our own. If you are like me, there are certain stories or certain characters in your inner dialogue. Some characters are positive. They encourage us, saying, "Yes, you can do that." Other characters are not positive; they bend to external pressures. These characters say, "Go with the flow. It's better to comply."

C. Otto Scharmer, in his seminal work, *Theory U*, discusses our inner voices of judgment, cynicism, and fear. It boils down to this: If I have an idea, and I want to try something new, one of my inner voices judges the idea good or bad. If I have a colleague, and she approaches me with a new concept she wants to work on together, one of my inner voices will judge her proposal. It may consider the proposal a risk, and so fear tells me to say no. Or my inner cynic may persuade me that the new concept will never work, and so I decline based on the false reality I've created.

The voice of judgment weighs in on an idea as advantageous or disadvantageous. The voice of cynicism tells me the idea will not work, and it provides reasons why. The voice of fear goes beyond both judgment and cynicism. It goes to a place of irrational belief. It says, "If you do this, if you move forward on this idea and take this risk, not only is it a bad idea that will not work, but something bad will happen to you as a result."

The voices of judgment, cynicism, and fear are inside us. We can try not to listen to them, but seldom do they go away altogether. Our answer to them lies is figuring out a way to resist and counteract them with more positive inner voices as we move along the path of ultra leadership.

A third challenge many people on the path to ultra leadership face is the ego and its drive for power. The ego wields tremendous power in our organizations. When we are "climbing the ladder of success" and move into more prominent roles, we assume that each step up means more power. Power feeds the ego. We end up trapped. We become more of a boss than a leader because we like being in control and having power, and we maintain this position by adhering to the status quo. Unfortunately, when we are more boss than leader, and our teams do our bidding simply because they are subordinate to our titles or positions, this breeds disengagement almost immediately. People do what we say because we tell them to, not because they are willingly and enthusiastically engaged and wanting to contribute their best. People don't want to work for a boss; they want to follow a leader. Many people in leadership, however, mistakenly think being a boss is easier, or more expedient, even though it ends up being counterproductive.

In sum, when we act as bosses instead of as leaders, we experience the results of our accidental design, our very own hamster wheel. We end up succumbing to external and internal challenges, complying with the pressure to conform, the need for speed. We end up listening to our internal voices telling us to stay on the beaten path; the power game motivates us, we let our egos drive us, and we just keep running and running and running. But it's not like running in an ultra marathon, because we do not keep a good pace, and there is a lack of support. It's a hamster wheel that just keeps on spinning. I've worked with many leaders in this situation. One day they wake up, usually in their late forties or early fifties, and wonder, "My God, why am I doing this?" Most times, they truly do not know why. It's a hard realization. If you're there now, it's time to step off the hamster wheel. If you're not there yet, take this opportunity to ensure that you never do.

When we are faced with obstacles to our growth as leaders, when we are at the edge of our competency, we must push farther. The edge, in all its many forms, can be specific or metaphorical. Seth Godin wrote that "edges are how we define things, they are the moments when things begin and end. The concept of the edge applies to every project, every concept, every institution in our lives. The edge of performance, the promises and goals we make every day, defines who we are and what we do. Most often we exist somewhere in the middle, but we gain understanding by going to the edge, pushing past it."

Each of us has an edge of confidence, comfort, and competence. I grew up believing I was not an athlete. As an adult, I saw people running ultra marathons and thought, *There is no way I could do that.* I held on to this belief born in a lack of confidence, and it became a comfort zone. It set limits on what I could accomplish, on what I would try and not try. Some limits are real. When I first decided to run an ultra marathon, I was not physically prepared to run 125 miles. Other limits are imagined, such as my thinking that I was not an athlete. But I decided I could push past those limits, to the edge of my ability. I prepared. I brought forward real change.

Leadership has an edge. Leaders only have so much knowledge and skill. Our edges of competence and confidence define the boundaries of our comfort zones. Lakota elder and teacher Buck Ghosthorse said, "Sometimes we have to travel to the edge of ourselves to find our center." To be ultra leaders, we need to own our reality, go to our edges, and push farther.

Developing the will to push the limits, and the skills to get people to engage and contribute, requires that we embark on a journey of personal growth. In doing so, we learn that we are not victims of circumstance. Viktor Frankl, who wrote *Man's Search for Meaning*, taught us that we choose our response to circumstances. Leading change and engaging others is a never-ending, iterative process.

The reality is that, until we improve leadership, we will not be able to address the failure rate for our change efforts or our employee engagement challenges with any lasting impact. At the end of the day, the only person I can truly change is me. In *The Fifth Discipline*, Peter Senge wrote about personal mastery. He said, "Personal mastery goes beyond competence and skills. It means approaching one's life as a creative work, living life from a creative as opposed to a reactive viewpoint." This philosophy is at the core of ultra leadership. It's what is missing from our current experience of leadership: the will to take the hero's journey to personal mastery and ultra leadership.

In our work with adult learners and leaders in particular, we have deployed a three-step process of learning and development that consistently holds true in helping individuals and groups to accelerate their development and learn a new way of being and leading. Learning that sticks and real personal development occurs when we engage in honest self-reflection and dialogue with others, and commit to practicing new ways of behaving and leading. Self-reflection is critical to developing self-awareness and becoming an ultra leader. It was Socrates who said, "The unexamined life is not worth living." There's power and truth in these words, especially if we want to lead others in important work.

And self-reflection is not enough. True, we become more self-aware through reflection, but our ability to act on a newfound awareness is strengthened and enhanced through dialogue with other people. When we engage another person in conversation about what we are discovering along the path to greater consciousness and leadership, we tend to gain an even deeper understanding of who we are and how we perform as leaders. Through dialogue, we can check our perceptions. The leaders I work with know that I will push them to engage with someone they trust in conversation regularly and ask for feedback about how they are performing. There is plenty of rationale for soliciting feedback on a regular basis. We need input and others' perspectives to explore and measure the gap between what we intend and what others are experiencing under our leadership. The fact is, if we are not open to feedback, we are not on the path to ultra leadership. When we stop learning, we stop leading. Reflection and dialogue provide data we can use to make adjustments.

Author Joseph Campbell wrote, "The hero's journey is one of the universal patterns through which that radiance shows brightly. What I think is that a good life is one hero journey after another. Over and over again you are called to the realm of adventure; you are called to new horizons. Each time there is the same problem: do I dare? And then if you do dare, the dangers are there and the help also, and the fulfillment or the fiasco. There's always the possibility of a fiasco, but there's also the possibility of bliss."

How does this apply to leadership? The hero is willing to go to the edge and push farther, over and over again. The best leaders share this willingness and embody the hero's nature. They are driven and called to new horizons. Ultra leadership is the willingness to push toward new horizons. Combine that desire in a leader with the skills to get people to join in, and opportunities abound. Leaders understand the possibility of failure, but turning back or maintaining the status quo is not an option. Every day, in every meeting and every interaction, we are called to leadership. In every moment, the question remains: Do I dare?

Do you demonstrate a will to push the limits? Consider the following descriptions of a leader who seeks out new horizons. Are they true for you?

1. I use personal power rather than authority to engage others.
2. I do not hesitate to cut through red tape to achieve success.
3. I will step in and lead when I encounter a void.
4. I convey a strong sense of urgency, asking myself, *What is of pressing importance?*
5. I encourage others to stretch beyond what they believe they can do.
6. I am comfortable with uncertainty.
7. I seek feedback from others on my impact and performance at least once a month.
8. I like to push the limits.

Hopefully you recorded yes for most answers. Then again, how do you know if you meet these criteria? See point 7.

CHAPTER THREE

Be Conscious, Connected, and Concerned

THINK ABOUT your first day at a new job. When you arrived, you were 100 percent engaged, willing and eager to contribute. In most cases, as time goes by, that engagement dwindles. Then it begins to tick down even more. On the second day, it might be 98 percent. Then something happens, and it drops down lower. Time goes by, things happen, and gradually your engagement rate is a fraction of what it once was. Why? Any number of factors: The work didn't appeal to your unique purpose, the culture was not open, the team you worked with was unorganized, or your manager was dismissive. Any one of these may have caused the drop in your engagement.

More times than not, people cite their manager as the reason for their drop in engagement and their eventual departure from an organization. The cost of low engagement to the US economy is staggering: $450 billion to $550 billion per year.

The ultra leadership mind-set shows leaders a way to combat low engagement by getting in front of it. Ultra leaders choose to be conscious, which means actively engaging their teams. Doing so sets a standard, and it displays a willingness to connect with and be concerned for other people. Being an ultra leader means being intentional about the development of others and our own leadership development. By growing and changing our mind-sets, and creating a better way of operating as a person, we can elevate the work environment to a place that inspires willing, enthusiastic, and sustained engagement.

BE CONSCIOUS

Being more conscious is a cornerstone of ultra leadership. It means being genuine and self-aware. In conversations and meetings, it means being mindful and fully present. There is also an aspect of consciousness that includes the capacity for high-level thinking. Since nearly 95 percent of our decision-making occurs in our subconscious minds, it is important for ultra leaders to be self-aware. Being self-aware leads to higher-level thinking. Higher-level thinking leads to more conscious decisions.

Research conducted by C. S. Soon et al. in 2008 discovered that our brains are already subconsciously aware of a decision before we make the decision in actual consciousness. Such an autopilot process to decision-making can inhibit creativity and innovation, two of the attributes of ultra leadership we are trying to embody. Making decisions on autopilot can become our routine (think: "usual and ordinary").

Recent research by J. L. Voss and K. A. Paller suggests that the brain accesses stored information accumulated over a lifetime. It uses the information to make decisions quickly—so fast that we make the decision before we are conscious of making it. When we base our decisions on what we've experienced in the past, it not only prevents us from seeing the present decision clearly, but it subverts our ability to understand the consequences.

Ultra leaders run contrary to the autopilot, unconscious mind-set. In fact, an important step an ultra leader takes is toward short-circuiting the autopilot tendency. We do that when we examine and evaluate our existing mental models for problem-solving and decision-making and make adjustments when necessary to ensure we are thinking carefully.

But let's not get ahead of ourselves. There's an aspect of being more conscious that is simply about being more present and observant, two more of the attributes of practitioners of ultra leadership.

The notion of being more conscious, and self-aware, and genuine corresponds with the word mindfulness, which is prevalent in today's vernacular and becoming more commonplace in our organizations. To some extent, mindfulness and consciousness are the same. Mindfulness refers to an ability to maintain a moment-by-moment awareness of what we are thinking and feeling. It touches on what is happening emotionally, physiologically, and psychologically around us, and extends to the people around us, the environment we are in, even the world as a whole. As we become more conscious, more self-aware and mindful, we develop the capacity to be more present and observant as leaders.

When we are more self-aware and more conscious, we can rely on who we are as individuals and less on our titles or positions. When we lead with this mind-set, we become less of a boss and more of a leader.

David Messenger, CEO and cofounder of Mast Mobile, said:

I think there is a difference between being conscious and unconscious as a leader. The unconscious leader is effectively a manager. The unconscious leader engages with a process, metrics, and tangibles—things that are predefined. Making the conscious decision to act as a leader is a fundamental shift in perspective. You are choosing to be yourself as much as anything else. I think authenticity is one of the key elements of someone who is a conscious leader. If you're working from an unconscious place, you are most likely making work, rather than doing work.

Striving to become more authentic and conscious is a decision we must make—consciously. When reflecting on who we are, we must decide if we're open to what we might find, and if we are open to change. Being open to what we find and open to change requires a capacity for self-affirmation. Self-affirmation is our ability to affirm our being—who we are—despite the doubt, anxiety, or external pressures that tell us not to change, and to just to go along.

In his poem, "The Self-Slaved," Patrick Kavanagh wrote:

Me I will throw away.
Me sufficient for the day
The sticky self that clings
Adhesions on the wings.

To love and adventure
To go on the grand tour
A man must be free
From self-necessity.

Greater consciousness enables self-affirmation, regardless of the doubts we may feel, the weaknesses we may discover, or the pressure to stop we may encounter. Can we live continuously self-reflective lives and keep the lines of communication with our inner lives open? Are we willing to drop ourselves, to get out of our own way, and to take a step toward ultra leadership? The question is: Can we live our life and lead others "without self-necessity"? It's a crucial question, and we must ask it of ourselves again and again so as not to forget.

When we do get out of the way, we live more consciously and bring ourselves more fully to our relationships and work as leaders. Janet Widmann is CEO of Kids Care Dental. Formerly she was the Executive Vice President of Markets at Blue Shield of California. Janet said:

> *A conscious leader is someone who is literally and metaphorically leaning in. They have decided they are going to lead. They're going to lead in all aspects of their professional life. A leader I worked with once said that more often than not, in a room full of his peers, when confronted with a challenge,*

most people would not lean in, but lean out. Now this leader,
regardless of whether it is in his area of direct accountability,
leans in and says, 'I am going to lead this. I am going to pick
this up and take on this challenge.' There is an intentional
and conscious decision, one that demonstrates the mind-
set of ultra leaders and the need to consistently upend the
ordinary, the business-as-usual approach.

Ultra leaders engage in honest self-reflection. Self-re-flection brings about self-awareness or consciousness that grows our capacity for self-affirmation. The desire to live and lead from a place of greater self-knowledge is the first element of the ultra leadership mind-set. But be warned. Robert Greenleaf, the founder of the servant leadership movement, observed, "Awareness is not a giver of solace—it is just the opposite. It is a disturber and awakener. Able leaders are usually sharply awake and reasonably disturbed. They are not seekers of solace. They have inner security." Our capacity for ultra leader-ship begins and ends with our decision to take the hero's journey to greater self-awareness and consciousness.

Why is becoming more conscious and self-aware import-ant? You only need to follow the data to see that becoming more conscious and self-aware is crucial to business suc-cess. A recent study conducted by The Korn Ferry Institute demonstrates that companies with a greater percentage of self-aware employees consistently outperformed those with a lower percentage (David Zes and Dana Landis, 2013). The study found that "poorly performing companies' employees had 20% more blind spots than those working at financially strong companies," and "poor performing companies' employees were 79% more likely to have low overall self-awareness than those at firms with robust ROR (rate of return)."

Greater consciousness and self-awareness enables us to live and lead with greater authenticity and intention. The study by Zes and Landis illustrates the benefits to the organization as well as the individual leader. When we encourage leaders to grow their self-awareness and become more conscious, we create a development culture and learning organization that will, in turn, improve individual, team, and organizational performance.

When we become more self-aware, we grow our capacity for greater self-management and self-determination. In the end, we become more authentic and impactful leaders, and the data shows benefits at the macro level of an organization as well. Organizations that encourage leaders to grow in self-awareness and foster a culture of ongoing learning and development (not just training) are building competitive advantage.

Peter Drucker wrote, "One does not manage people. The task is to lead people. The goal is to make productive the specific strengths and knowledge of every individual." Drucker's quotation lines up with Arie de Gues, who said that it is the role of leadership to "create the conditions in which people voluntarily give their best." To accomplish this, a leader relies not on his position or title, but on personal influence. The person in a leadership position is not necessarily more important, or better. The leader simply has a different role to inspire and enable the willing, enthusiastic, and repeated engagement and best contribution of others.

To be successful in this role, the ultra leader has the mind-set that tells him to be connected. The ultra leader knows that business happens as a result of relationships between people. There is no business-to-business or business-to-consumer. There is only human to human. By understanding connectedness, we make becoming more authentically connected a priority. When we do, we establish trust, encourage cooperation, and invite the collaboration necessary for aligned decision-making, creativity, and innovation to have a home in our organizations.

Robert Rigby-Hall, CEO of Beacon Global Group, former EVP/CHRO for NXP Semiconductors, and SVP/CHRO at LexisNexis Group, said:

I think it comes down to being authentic and desiring a connection. Genuinely care about people. That's the way the best leaders get the most out of people. They know their people. They know them at a personal level. They're easy to talk to and they view the time spent getting to know people as an important investment of their time. Part of that is revealing who you are as a leader and person. As I reflect back, one of the things that I was less good about and have worked on since was being open and showing who I was as a person. I was reasonably good at managing a team and then I got some feedback where people said, 'We don't really know who you are.' That feedback led me to consider how I might move from engaging unconsciously to more conscious leadership, appropriately revealing more of who I am in a more open way.

In 2004 in *Harvard Business Review*, Abraham Zaleznik wrote, "A managerial culture emphasizes rationality and control." That's usual and ordinary. Ultra leadership builds a culture that is vastly different. When our consciousness grows, one of the things we discover is our continual and inescapable connection with others. We then strive to create a culture around us that reflects our discovery.

People know how and when they are being measured extrinsically, solely for what they produce. In this regard, the leader's relationship with them is transactional: "Do this thing for me, and you and I will be in good standing." When people are valued intrinsically, as individuals, regardless of what they produce, the relationship is not transactional. It exists for its own sake. It is about creating and maintaining a connection. Our recognition of connection and demonstration of concern communicates that the value we have for the individual, whether she is a direct report, stakeholder, or customer, is intrinsic. When people experience this concern, they do not feel disposable. They feel they are important to the organization and to the leader. This approach is always superior to measuring people by extrinsic value alone.

I believe part of the reason we see such poor engagement numbers in organizations today has to do with people feeling that they are measured extrinsically. If I am an employee, and my leader does not have a connection with me; if he only measures me by what I produce; if he does not desire an authentic relationship with me—all of these things lead me to believe that I am disposable. As a disposable employee, I am only going to do what I must do to get by, not more. I am certainly not going to willingly, enthusiastically, and repeatedly engage and contribute.

On the other hand, if my leader is conscious, connected, and concerned, I feel valued and part of the team. I want nothing more than to produce high-quality work, day after day. Some may discount this mind-set as being part of the "soft skills" department. But it is tremendously important to building leadership capacity in an organization that is not reactive, but rather able to connect with people and to be responsive to their needs.

It is our connection with others and our demonstration of real concern for them that inspires willing, enthusiastic, and repeated engagement. Being conscious and connected means having empathy for people that manifests as genuine concern for their welfare and happiness. We understand that others are a part of our lives and work. We cannot hope to engage others without seeking and maintaining a real connection and authentically inviting them into our circle of concern.

For years, I've encountered individuals and groups who, when I advocate for becoming more conscious, connected, and concerned, attempt to discount the message or negate its importance to their situation. Many want to jump right to the trick or technique for going faster, selling more, or doing more. They want a shortcut, an escalator to the top of Hope Pass. There isn't one.

The work of leadership succeeds or fails on our level of self-awareness and our ability to engage each moment and person mindfully and consciously. All the tools or techniques in the world won't help if we don't know if, when or how to use them. We don't stand a chance in you-know-where to inspire willing, enthusiastic, and repeated engagement without acknowledging our connection with others and demonstrating that connection through our authentic concern for who they are intrinsically. We cannot drive real change without the strong engagement and contributions of others. If you want to succeed in moving the business from point A to point B, in driving real change, then you must work daily to become more conscious, connected, and concerned in order to inspire willing, enthusiastic, and repeated engagement.

Why? In 2001, the Hay Group found that companies with high engagement levels reported a 2.5 times revenue increase. What's more, the Corporate Executive Board of 2004 demonstrated that there is an 87 percent decrease in the likelihood or departure of highly engaged employees in companies with high engagement. When you consider the cost of replacing folks, keeping employees engaged presents huge savings. A 2012 study by Custom Insight found that 49 percent of US workers cited problems with direct supervisors as the number one reason for disengagement. This study underscores the fact that, while engagement is a dire problem in need of fixing, it is leadership, the direct supervisors causing employees' disengagement, that we must focus on and overhaul. That's why we're here.

There is no shortcut. The tools and techniques you encounter in this book or elsewhere are useless unless you commit to the daily practice and lifelong journey of becoming more conscious, connected, and concerned as a leader.

Consider the following statements. Are they true for you?

- I am aware of my emotional state.
- I am not preoccupied with the past or future.
- I can remain focused and calm in the midst of swirl.
- I quickly catch myself when I am working on autopilot.
- If I need something, I have people who will help me.
- I have solid relationships with friends and colleagues.
- I am part of a larger community.
- I take time to know what's going on in the lives of my team members and colleagues.
- I am upset when I see someone being treated poorly.
- When those around me are happy or sad, I become happy or sad as well.
- I find it easy to see another person's perspective.
- I notice the moods and feelings of others.

The daily practice of being conscious, connected, and concerned as a leader means getting to a strong "yes" for each of these statements. The good news is that every minute, every meeting, and every day is a "do over." Keep trying.

CHAPTER FOUR

Think Carefully

LEADERSHIP ACUMEN is not the same thing as business acumen. Many of us possess comprehensive business knowledge. We may know much about our particular market or product or service, but our leadership muscles are in need of a workout. As we forge a new path toward ultra leadership, we must first acknowledge the need for a new way forward.

We must be willing to admit that unconscious or careless decision-making has serious unintended and detrimental consequences for our teams and organizations. The economic impact of careless thinking is evident in the engagement and change statistics cited earlier. We must be prepared to admit, when it comes to certain attributes and skills of leadership, that we sometimes remain unconscious of our incompetence. If we look at the success rates of organizational change and employee engagement, it is plain to see that, when we talk about leadership, we may not be as capable as we think.

In 1970, Noel Burch of Gordon Training International developed a theory positing that *unconscious incompetence* is actually the first stage of competence. At this juncture of competence, we don't know how to do something, and we aren't aware of our deficit. When we recognize that we have a deficit, we move to the second stage of *conscious incompetence*. Now that we are aware that we do not know something, and as we work to develop our knowledge and skill, we begin to grow our *conscious competence*, which is the third stage of competence. At stage three, we know how to do something, but doing that thing requires focused attention and intention. Finally comes the fourth stage. In the fourth stage of *unconscious competence*, we have had so much practice doing something that it has become second nature; the task is completed efficiently and expertly.

Of course, there is always room for improvement. The best athletes, actors, painters, and so on all reflect on their work and strive to improve everyday. Many work with a coach or mentor or teacher, and together they practice their craft. This is the only way to move into a place of conscious and eventually unconscious competence. The same principles hold true for leadership. The best leaders are constantly—to borrow a phrase from Steven Covey—"sharpening the saw." In other words, as leaders, we need to stay open to the possibility that we are not always as great as we think. Such self-appraisal and objectivity reinforces the need for consistent feedback. Find a colleague you trust, and ask him or her to tell you how you are doing in your leadership role. Are you thinking carefully and allowing room for creativity and innovation? Are you feeling fully, in a way that supports good self-management and interaction with others? Are you communicating effectively to engage others with clarity and inspire their best contributions?

Consider the myriad leadership competencies you have been asked to develop over the years. Line them up horizontally from left to right. They represent one axis of leadership development: problem-solving, decision-making, influencing, planning, delegating, financial analyzing, presenting, coaching, giving feedback, listening, inquiring, team managing, negotiating, visioning, strategic thinking, organizing, collaborating—the list goes on and on. We learn these competencies through leadership training. Think of the competencies on this horizontal axis as the applications of effective leadership. We rely on these apps to help us successfully navigate various circumstances and situations.

It is important to develop these apps, and the techniques associated with applying them, but what about the operating system that runs them? After all, some apps do not run on old, antiquated operating systems. To run the numerous apps associated with leadership, we must update our personal operating system regularly. How? By focusing attention on a vertical axis of leadership development and encouraging personal, cognitive, and emotional growth in addition to adding apps through competency training along the horizontal axis. When we take a multidimensional approach to leadership development, by integrating horizontal axis training and vertical axis development, we increase our ability to push the limits and inspire others to come with us.

Ginger Crowne, who heads up Talent Development and Leadership Development at Veritas, told me:

> *The challenges will only continue to grow. We need leaders to keep pace in terms of their personal, cognitive, and emotional development. Moving forward, leadership development must challenge and support leaders to widen their development to grow on both axes. For too long leadership development has skimmed across the surface. Those of us who support leaders and their teams have to demonstrate leadership ourselves and push back when we get asked to do something that we know is a tick-the-box*

approach to development and won't make a difference in the life of the leader or the team. It's our job to help them go deeper where and when they need to.

A multidimensional approach includes developing a foundational mind-set and skill set that enables us to appropriately leverage all other leadership competencies. Only a multifaceted approach ensures that we make the necessary shift and develop a competence for ultra leadership. A multifaceted approach to leadership development means encouraging leaders to make the intentional decision to step out of their comfort zones of competence—be it as engineers, marketers, finance directors, or salespersons—and to undertake the journey to conscious competence with thinking carefully, feeling fully, and communicating effectively in order to engage others and drive real change. These skills enable the appropriate and masterful application of all other leadership skills and competencies.

Let's begin by reviewing the foundational skill set of ultra leadership with a reminder that the mind-set, the desire to be conscious and lead, is critical to any work that develops and hones the skills required to go beyond usual and ordinary. Our mind-set and the foundational skills of ultra leadership make up the personal operating system upon which we build our leadership capacity. We need a particular level of consciousness to know if, when, and how to use the various tools and techniques we acquire as we grow our leadership competencies.

We have all been on the receiving end of well-intentioned leaders who, fresh from a training event covering a skill or tool, allow that tool to become the go-to answer for every wrong a team, colleague, or direct report experiences. When we grow our personal operating system, which consists of an ultra leader's mind-set and foundational skill set, we know if, how, and when to use, not just new tools, but all the instruments and techniques they possess in their tool kit.

If we want to push the limits, drive business from point *A* to point *B*, and move people from engaging as groups to being high-performing teams, we must develop ourselves from managing on autopilot to leading with intention. It is our responsibility as leaders to recognize and overcome stasis personally and in our organizations and teams. We must go to the edge and push farther, over and over again, and transform the status quo, so that our teams and organizations achieve success. To do this, we must think more carefully.

The problem, however, is that careful thinking is not easy or automatic, and it does not come to most people naturally. For most of us, our thoughts focus on the short-term, on what's next. We think about the tasks before us today, and those we need to complete in a week, month, or quarter. Nobel Laureate Daniel Kahneman refers to this tendency, to only see what is in front of us, as the "spotlight" effect. What's more, when our thinking is undisciplined, we are reactive and influenced by our inability to feel fully, to understand and manage our emotions. Another factor that hampers our ability to think carefully is age. As we age, we tend to lose our curiosity. We become knowers instead of learners. We become the proverbial hammer seeing nails in every situation. These tendencies—our short-term focus, emotional reactivity, and lack of curiosity—combine to thwart our desire and ability to think carefully and strategically.

The combined implication of these tendencies is that we experience a gap between strategic thinking and intelligent action. We succumb to a pattern of thinking and acting that is careless and counterproductive to driving successful change. We tend toward the obvious and the expedient. When we are unable to think carefully and plan strategically, we rely on old solutions for current situations, resulting in a "ready, fire, aim" mentality—aiming only after we have already fired. This tendency has become part of our corporate cultures and is detrimental to our efforts to innovate, cause positive disruption, and lead change. The "ready, fire, aim" mentality has become ingrained in our way of working as individuals and teams.

A grave consequence of the "ready, fire, aim" mentality is that, while we may think we are moving fast and efficiently, we are actually static, fixed in time and space. We have come to confuse busy-ness with business. As long as this pattern continues, the gap between careful thinking, strategic thinking, and decisive action grows wider. *McKinsey Quarterly* sponsored a survey of more than two thousand executives, and only 28 percent said that the quality of strategic decision-making within their organizations was satisfactory. Sixty percent thought bad decisions occurred as frequently as good ones. The remaining 12 percent felt that right decisions were altogether infrequent.

Even when leaders believe they are thinking carefully, they may be evaluating their competence unconsciously and inaccurately. Dan Lovallo and Olivier Sibony studied more than one thousand major business decisions over a span of five years. They looked at the role of analysis and process in decision-making. Their research indicated that "process mattered more than analysis by a factor of six."

We now know that careless thinking has dire consequences for teams and organizations. We are aware that we must be conscious and employ careful thinking at all times. But what does careful thinking look like—what does it entail?

Careful thinking involves being able to encounter confusion, hold multiple pieces of information in our memories at any given moment, analyze each piece of information, and understand the relationship among all that information to lessen the confusion. Careful thinking also involves generating and considering new and creative opportunities to address challenges and to prioritize based on strategic value. The ultra leadership attributes of being present and observant support our intention to lessen the confusion.

If you have ever assembled an item purchased at Ikea, you have a sense of what it is to experience confusion and strive to find meaning there, with all of those parts spread out, waiting for you to put them together. Finding meaning in confusion requires the ability for organization. Organization is the capacity to dissemble an issue, look at the pieces, and then reconstitute it and organize it into new ideas.

Organization requires logical inquiry. We use this skill all the time without realizing it because, in each moment, we are making decisions. Useful and productive decision-making requires organizational ability. We must be able to examine carefully a problem, situation, challenge, or opportunity from all sides, and then put it all back together in the form of a solution. It is never good to have leftover parts when assembling something. "Leave no stone unturned" is a mantra of a leader who is present, observant, and thinking carefully.

Another part of careful thinking is perspective. Great chess players, for example, see the whole board and are thinking multiple moves ahead of their current move. A capacity for perspective is what makes a chess master. It is also a hallmark of careful thinking because perspective generates opportunities. Having perspective means being able to hold a challenge, a problem, in mind, and to extend our thoughts not only to the past, where we can recall a previous solution, but also to the future, where we can imagine a new possible solution. The more careful our thinking, the greater our perspective becomes. We overcome the tendency to see only what we want to see or are prepared to see. Perspective enables us to avoid the trap of blindly applying old solutions to new situations.

To make a decision, we must learn the facts and then choose a course of action. The problem, unfortunately, is that most decision-making is based on previous experiences. We think, *What did I do before, in a similar situation?* But if leadership is responsible for driving change, decision-making based solely on existing information and past solutions is not up to the task. Real change and innovation are impossible under such circumstances. It's imperative that we anticipate multiple possibilities and be proactive in addressing potential implications and consequences. Doing so means looking at our assumptions and asking, "So what?" Perspective enables us to design the optimal way forward rather than the obvious. Simply reaching back into the past to address current and future business needs no longer suffices, and it falls into the category of usual and ordinary leadership. The way we think about something determines our actions and the direction we follow. It is true for us as individuals, teams, and organizations.

If careful thinking does not come naturally to us, how do we cultivate it on an organizational level? To develop careful reflection, we must examine the mental models on which we already rely. These models represent our thought processes. By asking ourselves, "What is my process of reflection? What steps do I usually take to arrive at decisions?" we come closer to understanding what Lovallo and Sibony meant when they said that process matters more than analysis. We encourage careful thinking by paying attention to different levels of perception, and doing so provides a foundation for evaluating our existing mental models. As a result, we create a more productive thought process. A learning process by which we consider existing information such as past solutions, carefully examine our current reality, and access our imagination to explore new possibilities is the single best way to implement careful thinking across an organization. The tool kit we'll discuss in chapter 7 includes a mental model to help facilitate careful thinking and cultivate it on an organizational level.

The authors of *Presence* (Peter Senge, et al.) interviewed Brian Arthur of the Santa Fe Institute for that fantastic book. In those interviews Arthur states that we have two types of cognition. The first involves applying existing information to a situation. He calls this "downloading." The second type of cognition includes "accessing inner-knowing," which not only taps into existing information, but also looks at the present moment and into the future for new opportunities. In those interviews Arthur shared a three-step process for what I consider conscious, careful thinking.

At the first step, we "observe, observe, observe." When we do this, we short-circuit our "ready, fire, aim" tendency. We pause our habit of downloading to pay attention. We have been told our entire lives by parents and teachers to pay attention, but it is striking how frequently many of us stop paying attention to what is going on around us and inside us. By observing and paying attention, we learn to aim before we fire, which requires us to be present. We have to be conscious and connected to engage others, and we must be observant and concerned about what is occurring in the field of our experience.

Being present and observant enables us to take the time to assess our current situation fully, to go through the process of organization before jumping into action. If our tendency is to download and then race from here to there, incorporating this first step in our thought and decision-making process helps us become more reflective and less impulsive. We can become more conscious of our individual purpose and more aligned with organizational expectations.

At the second step, Arthur says we must, "retreat and reflect and allow the inner knowing to emerge." It is at this step that we strive to be intensely curious about the realities and reasons for the situation at hand. When we are curious, we set aside our preconceived notions about our current situation. Being curious allows present and future possibilities to inform our thinking. At this second step, we engage our imaginations and consider all the options. We invite creativity and innovation, two attributes of ultra leadership, as we consider the advantages and disadvantages of a course of action before jumping into action. If we continue to be curious in our thinking and attitude, the possibilities multiply, and we imagine options that were never considered or experienced before. We create multiple paths for a best possible future.

The third step, according to Arthur, is about "acting in an instant." At this step, we want to start moving. We need to identify the most appropriate course of action. Taking the first two steps of observing and reflecting increases the likelihood that our thinking, now, at this third step, will move us in the right direction. Taking the time to aim before we fire increases the likelihood we will strike our target. Our thoughts help us put the pieces back together. It involves building a strategy and making plans. This third step is where we make conscious decisions about what to do and what not to do. As such, we engage people and tasks more purposefully.

As we grow this foundational skill of thinking carefully, we strengthen the ultra leadership attributes. We become more present and observant in every situation. We become more creative and innovative as we consider how best to engage others and drive change. We become more strategic and purposeful in our actions. Janet Widmann put it like this:

> We can go very fast. We pride ourselves on getting lots of stuff done in a short amount of time. It takes leadership

to think carefully, to stop when necessary and ask, 'Where are we? What are we trying to create or achieve? What are the possibilities for next steps?' It takes leadership to make sure we're being productive and not just busy. Careful thinking ensures we are connected to our mission and our purpose for going so fast and trying to get so much done. It is leadership informed by careful thinking that ensures we're being intentional with how we're spending our time and energy.

Consider the following statements about thinking carefully. Are they true for you?

- I can anticipate change and proactively plan to address potential objections and barriers.
- I question assumptions as part of my decision-making process.
- I'm able to see the underlying patterns that cause problems.
- I consider the organization's strategic intent when making decisions and prioritizing actions.
- I carefully compare and contrast multiple options and their possible outcomes before making a decision.
- I effectively prioritize to manage complex and competing tasks.
- I consider other people's perspectives and points of view when making decisions.
- I am open to learning new things.

Our ability to think carefully rests on how open and diligent we are about developing the second foundational skill of ultra leadership—feeling fully.

CHAPTER FIVE

Feel Fully

I KNOW that the term "feeling fully" may sound a little "woo-woo" or "touchy-feely" to some. I use it intentionally. More than twenty years of experience as a therapist, coach, and consultant make me confident in an observation that most of us are not completely in touch with or in control of the emotions that drive our behavior. I include myself in this assessment. Because we don't "feel fully," we aren't as conscious as we might want or need to be in order to manage the emotions associated with regularly and fully engaging others. We aren't as connected to others as we could be. This impacts our level of concern for others. Our ability to think carefully is not as strong as it might be. All of these things contribute to our becoming unconscious contributors to the usual and ordinary in our organizations, hindering our attempts to drive real change.

The path of ultra leadership requires that we focus on building the foundational skill of feeling fully. There is no turning back now. There is no stopping here. There is no work-around. It may feel like climbing to Hope Pass, but growing our capacity to feel fully will strengthen our capacity to think carefully and communicate effectively.

Back in chapter 1, we learned about one leader's change of heart concerning effective, healthy leadership. Early in his career, this leader thought that proper management consisted of processes, systems, and numbers, and that, for the most part, people were interchangeable. Simply by keeping his systems moving with people who could plug in numbers, he could keep his organization, his machine, running smoothly. Eventually, he realized that when he demonstrated real concern—when he valued his people intrinsically and not just for what they contributed—productivity, as well as engagement, increased considerably.

Unfortunately, much misguided management thinking is still pervasive in organizations today. It is this type of thinking that reinforces the idea that an organization is a machine that must not be disrupted. This thinking dissuades leaders from engaging in personal development to grow their capacity for feeling fully and, in turn, becoming ultra leaders.

What does it mean to feel fully? It means to be emotionally self-aware and capable of managing our emotions. It means managing our energy so we can positively engage and interact with others. Growing our capacity to feel fully correlates directly to the ultra leadership mind-set that leads us to be more conscious, connected, and concerned. Having a drive to lead should manifest partly in the desire to connect with others consciously and compassionately. If we accept this premise, then our conversation about feeling fully must begin with a look at what we are connecting to: our organizational system.

The metaphor of an organization as a machine no longer suits us. Machines are built for a purpose and then maintained over time. As we live in an era of continuous change, we need to shift our thinking regarding organizations. This change has been underway for a long time. In 1996, Margaret Wheatley wrote, "We want organizations to be adaptive, flexible, self-renewing, resilient, learning, intelligent—all attributes only found in living systems. The tension of our times is that we want our organizations to be healthy living systems, but we only know how to treat them as machines."

A system is a perceived whole. Its elements band together because they affect each other over time and operate toward a common purpose. The word *system* comes from the Greek verb *sunistC!nai,* which means, "to cause to stand together." Henry Ford said, "Coming together is a beginning; keeping together is progress; working together is success. Leadership that goes beyond usual and ordinary causes people to "stand together."" Without feeling fully, we cannot lead others to come together, stay together, and work together.

Everything from biological organisms to the universe is a system. Humans are also systems. Human-constructed groups are systems as well. The organization, the teams within it, and the people in the teams are all systems. Think of it as a Russian nesting doll. We are a system made of systems, living and working in a system, and so on.

Some people see the structure of an organization as synonymous with its organizational chart. Others think structure means the design of the organizational workflow and processes. From a systems perspective, the structure is the pattern of interrelationships among elements of the system. These elements include the hierarchy and process flows, attitudes and perceptions, the quality of products, the ways in which we make decisions, and any number of additional factors.

Systemic structures are often invisible until someone points them out. For example, at a large bank, whenever the efficiency ratio decreases by two points, departments are told to cut expenses and make layoffs. But when asked what the efficiency ratio means, bank employees typically say, "It's just a number we use. It doesn't affect anything." If you ask, "What would happen if that number were to change?" you begin to understand that every element is part of one or more fundamental structures.

The word *structure* comes from the Latin word *struere*, which means "to build." Structures in systems, however, are not necessarily developed consciously. Our structures are built as a result of the choices we make over time. Without developing the skill to feel fully, it is likely these choices are made unconsciously.

From a systemic perspective, structure refers to the web of relationships an organization relies on to sustain itself. When we as leaders examine our relationships with our direct reports, our peers, our customers, and our stakeholders, we begin to see how we have consciously or unconsciously structured our interactions and the impact of those choices on operational success or failure. When we engage in our work and others unconsciously, the more usual and ordinary our experience and results will be. But when we begin to see that our choices are the source of our successes and our failures, the desire to create a different way forward springs forth.

According to physicist Fritjof Capra, all living systems have three basic characteristics. First, they are capable of *autopoiesis*, which means they create themselves. Second, all systems are self-organizing and adaptive in ways distinctively different from their past. They experience "emergence." And third, all living systems are in some way aware of and capable of interacting with their environment; they can think.

Think of your organization as a living system. It created itself through the activities of its founders. It adapts to changes in the environment and organizes to sustain itself. Finally, it is aware of and able to interact with its environment, which is the dynamic global economy. Success or failure is determined by how aware it is and how quickly it adapts and organizes itself to re-create itself as a system within the larger system. Every organization, segment, region, work group, team, and individual that make up your organization has these three characteristics and is engaged in this same process at all times. Just like the organizational system, success or failure for an individual system, a person, depends on choices. Our choices are determined by our capacity to think carefully and feel fully.

We know that to think carefully we must feel fully. That's implied in Brian Arthur's challenge to us to "allow our inner knowing to emerge." We can think things through carefully only when we have developed a capacity for feeling fully, regulating our response to emotions and controlling our instincts to ensure our behavior is strategic and purposeful. Behavior refers to the actions or reactions of a system within its environment. Our behavior can be conscious or unconscious, overt or covert, voluntary or involuntary. Human behavior can be common, unusual, acceptable, or unacceptable. Humans evaluate the acceptability of behavior using social norms and regulate behavior by means of social control. In animals, behavior is controlled by the endocrine system and the nervous system. The complexity of the behavior of an organism is related to the complexity of its nervous system. Our behavior is more complex than an animal's. Generally, organisms with complex nervous systems have a greater capacity to learn new responses and thus adjust their behavior. That's good news for us as we work to shift our behavior and create a new paradigm of leadership.

All behavior has meaning. We do not continue behaviors that do not produce desired effects. It is important to keep in mind that there is no such thing as purposeless behavior. If someone is behaving a certain way, there is a reason for it. We think that our behavior is driven by cognition alone, but our decisions are made more times than not in our subconscious mind. Our instincts and emotions play an integral part in what we think of as rational decisions.

When threatened, we each have a default setting or first reaction. This is known as the "fright, flight, or fight" instinct. When we become frightened, our natural instinct is either to fight or to take flight. Watch people in a meeting and you'll see the "fright, flight, or fight" instinct at work. Watch how emotion takes over in those instances. When frustration grows or tempers flare or when a confrontation is occurring, notice who jumps in and who withdraws. Those reactions to the situation are instinctual and emotional.

Times of change in organizations are disruptive by nature and, as a result, evoke fear. As mentioned earlier, people fear the uncertainty associated with change. This pattern of behavior takes hold in an organization and can become the norm. Leaders who think carefully and feel fully are more likely to bring forward change that lasts and goes beyond usual and ordinary because they see the organization as a system and relate to it as such.

Going beyond usual and ordinary means seeing our organizations and the people within them as living systems to be engaged rather than machines to be maintained. It means continuously working to become more conscious, connected, and concerned. It means wanting to be aware of what drives our behavior and the behavior of others. This awareness, particularly self-awareness, is the foundation of emotional intelligence, and the key to feeling fully. David Messenger told me, "You can't overstate its importance. If the definition of a leader is getting people to follow you rather than complete a task for you, then a leader has to be emotionally engaged and invested in others. People need to have confidence in your ability to calmly navigate the challenges that may arise along the way. To me, emotional intelligence is fundamental in trying to get that done."

All thinking involves emotion. Our brains are hardwired to ensure that emotion is involved in decision-making as a survival instinct. The inability to perceive the realities of a situation, including the feelings and actions of others, can have devastating effects. Such a failure leads to a lack of poise or poor decision-making in a moment of crisis. Decisions that are driven by unregulated or uncontained emotion can have devastating effects. To ensure that our decisions and actions are appropriate to the situation, we must develop emotional intelligence.

Daniel Goleman is the leading voice on emotional intelligence. He defines it as "the ability to regulate one's response to emotion, manage the emotional impact on decision-making, read the emotions of others, and act appropriately in relationships." In fact, emotional intelligence may be more conducive to success than cognitive intelligence. According to Goleman, four inherent abilities collectively define emotional intelligence: self-awareness, self-management, social awareness, and relationship management.

Emotional intelligence begins with self-awareness. It is a lack of self-awareness that brings leaders down, limits growth, and topples organizations. The emotionally intelligent leader is aware of her emotions and the impact of emotions on behavior. She is also capable of accurate self-assessment, which enables her to seek help when needed, and to focus and follow through on personal-growth initiatives. Self-awareness creates confidence to accept challenges and to go beyond usual and ordinary.

A second key aspect of emotional intelligence is self-management. Critical to self-management is the capacity for self-regulation. As we expand our awareness of who we are, we grow the ability to lead ourselves and regulate our responses to emotion through self-dialogue. The regulation of emotional response is the capacity to contain our emotions, negative or positive, and remain calm in charged situations. For example, think about the last time someone cut you off on the freeway. Most likely you got angry. By regulating your emotional response, you are able to be aware that you are upset and to shut the anger down. You are angry for a moment, not the rest of the day. The regulation of emotional response is essential if careful thinking is to occur. It enhances our ability to recall past experiences and to be observant of our current reality, patiently engaging in organization, extending our perspective, and imagining multiple future options while working through a problem and making a decision. Without a capacity for the regulation of emotional response, we stay stuck in a false sense of urgency that we create under the belief that all we need to do is download a solution quickly, and then move forward. A keen ability for emotional self-regulation also supports our capacity to organize complex situations and initiate appropriate work.

Self-management is characterized by transparency, adaptability, achievement, initiative, and optimism. The self-managing person transparently lives his or her values, adapts to challenging situations, pragmatically works to achieve goals, and is an optimistic self-starter. Self-management enables the ability to get started on, pay attention to, and finish work. It is the ability to focus on a task or a series of tasks and sustain the required level of care over an extended period of time, even when the work is less than stimulating.

To manage complexity as an organization evolves, leaders must be adept at self-management., able to initiate projects without external influence, direction, or instruction, while remaining open to supportive interaction and dialogue. Strong self-management creates an ability to discern what deserves initiation and follow through. It provides a groundedness that enables a leader to self-impose a structure and a discipline to allow the corporate entrepreneurial vision to be realized.

We develop our capacity to self-manage through the learning process mentioned earlier: reflection, dialogue, and practice. With regard to emotional intelligence and feeling fully, this self-management begins when we engage in an inner conversation that assists in guiding our behavior and directing our future actions. Our internal desire for self-awareness and self-leadership drives our self-dialogue. The pace of business is fast. If our first instinct is to act without reflecting, results are impacted negatively. Our capacity for self-dialogue will strengthen our ability to slow ourselves down just enough to respond effectively and carefully to the unique demands of each situation.

The emotionally intelligent person is also socially aware. She is empathetic and can tune into and respond to the emotions of others. She is aware of the social and political realities of the groups and organization in which she operates. Social awareness involves fostering an emotional climate that supports healthy relationships within and between groups and organizations. From a business perspective, social awareness pays close attention to organizational engagement and maintains healthy internal and external relationships with colleagues and customers alike.

Lastly, emotional intelligence involves an aptitude for relationship management, which entails the ability to inspire, influence, and develop others. It means being a driver of positive change, and being able to handle conflicts as they arise in that disruption. A strong capacity for relationship management enables us to better foster teamwork, inspire cooperation, and facilitate strong collaboration.

On March 15, 2004, the *Los Angeles Times* noted of Goleman: "His own reviews of data involving business and government leaders suggest that the most successful people have a strong sense of how emotions affect their decisions and workplace relationships. 'What you see in these star performers that you don't see as often in average managers are emotional competencies: empathy, sensitivity, whether the person's tuned in, can cooperate well, takes initiative. Technical skill is important—but you can hire other people to do that.'"

It is impossible to overstate the importance of emotional intelligence as a foundational skill for leaders. Recent research conducted by Travis Bradbury and TalentSmart indicate that 90 percent of top performers in organizations have high emotional intelligence. Janet Widmann summarized the concept nicely:

> *I find emotional intelligence is still all too rare. Those who have it—it really does separate them from the rest. That self-awareness and ability to work with others gives you the opportunity to get folks to give discretionary effort. People have choices about what to do with their time and energy. Your emotional intelligence helps you convey that you care about them personally and professionally, and that leads people to engage and contribute. Emotional intelligence helps you understand the unspoken environment that is happening around you. Feeling fully makes you a more efficient leader. Your ability to connect with other people is what keeps a high-performing team in place.*

Peter Andrade added, "Emotional intelligence is the most important element of my job, and is one of, if not the key, differentiator in the performance of senior leaders."

In chapter 3, I proposed that being conscious—that is, self-aware—is the keystone of the ultra leadership mind-set. In the same way, and as stated at the beginning of this chapter, the ability to feel fully is absolutely vital to being able to think carefully and communicate effectively. Feeling fully manifests as being conscious, connected, and concerned. The mind-set and skill set of ultra leadership are multipliers. Take out one element, and we're back to the usual and ordinary.

Consider the following statements about feeling fully. Are they true for you?

- I recognize how my emotions drive behaviors that impact my performance.
- I have a strong capacity for managing my counterproductive impulses.
- I can easily talk about my feelings.
- I easily adapt to new challenges, adjusting my thinking and behavior in the face of change.
- I am a self-starter, able to take action and follow through.
- I have regular physical, emotional, and mental practices that keep me resilient.
- My core values guide my decisions in complex situations.
- I can sense what others are feeling and can demonstrate empathy toward them.
- I seek feedback from others on my impact and performance at least once a month.

The path to going beyond usual and ordinary is a journey inward. There is no way around. There is no shortcut. Developing the ultra leadership mind-set and these foundational skills is a daily practice and lifelong journey to find our edges and push farther.

CHAPTER SIX

Communicate Effectively

BEFORE WE DISCUSS how to communicate effectively, let's examine the costs of miscommunication. Miscommunication may be the leading cause of resistance to change. It's responsible for late, over-budget, and failed initiatives. In short, ineffective communication is a prime contributor to our current reality of low engagement and failed change efforts. Companies with effective communication policies, behaviors, and practices are 50 percent more likely to report turnover levels below industry averages. That's compared to 33 percent in cases where communication is less effective. The study, conducted by Watson Wyatt, indicated that when leaders communicate effectively, and keep employees well informed, absence rates are below average.

A recent survey by Towers Watson revealed that only three out of ten employees say their manager is effective at dealing with resistance to change. What's more, in a survey conducted by a US association of IT professionals, 28 percent of respondents cited poor communication as the primary cause of project failure, causing two out of every three projects ever begun to fail. The Towers Watson survey concluded that companies with highly effective communication practices experienced 47 percent higher total returns to shareholders, compared to organizations with less effective communication policies, behaviors, and practices.

A leading cause of miscommunication is our failure to realize that the quality and quantity of our communication is inadequate. Psychologists call this tendency *signal amplification bias*. This means that we overestimate how much, through our words and deeds, we are communicating. We assume others will fill in our communication gaps. I speak from personal experience. Because of my own preference to go fast, I am guilty of this ineffective communication habit. I assumed that my team members knew what I meant and would respond accordingly in how they engaged and contributed to our work. My coach pointed out that, while my team was exceptional, none of them were great at mind reading. If I wanted something from an individual or the entire team, I needed to overcome my tendency for signal amplification bias and communicate more effectively.

Another cause of miscommunication is the tendency to act based on faulty assumptions. We see something, we attribute meaning based on existing information, and then we take action. Most assumptions are wrong. One might say miscommunication stems from careless thinking. We react within the moment, with no curiosity about what we are experiencing or why.

Emotional reactivity is another cause of miscommunication. When we are triggered emotionally, we say and do things we later wish we could take back. I know I am guilty of this, and most likely you are, too. Emotional reactivity is a sign that we are not feeling fully.

Ineffective communication due to careless thinking and not feeling fully contributes to a lack of alignment among people and teams. If we hope to be more successful in leading change, both leaders and teams must be engaged and contribute their best work. To do this, we must align with a clear vision and strategy. We must align with the plan to execute strategy and identify an individual's role and responsibilities. We must clearly understand how we measure success and evaluate the shared experience of working together.

When we are not aligned, we say and do things that communicate confusion. Keith Mitchell, Partner, EMEIA Business Development Leader at Ernst and Young, believes that "communicating effectively begins with being present enough to know what you're saying is being understood and accepted, and respecting the fact that we may not yet be on the same page with others. If not, we need to inquire and listen to make sure we are as clear as possible and that we are aligned." To that end, we must develop better ways to communicate to lessen confusion, create alignment, and inspire engagement.

As mentioned, there is no business-to-business or business-to-consumer. There is only human to human. Business is conducted via relationships, which is why ultra leadership flows from the mind-set of consciousness, connection, and concern. Philosopher Martin Buber said, "All real living is meeting." Communicating effectively is foundational to ultra leadership because relationships begin and endure through communication that determines how well we can meet another person.

Conversation matters. I consider it an axiom of business that conversation is a core business process. Juanita Brown and David Isaacs, co-originators of the World Cafe, first suggested this idea back in the 1990s. They said, "Thoughtful conversations around questions that matter might be the core process in any company—the source of organizational intelligence that enables the other business processes to create positive results."

Conversations are taking place right now in your organization. Some are taking place face-to-face, others virtually. Some are via text, phone, and email. People at every level are sharing information that is critical to your business. These conversations are based on careful thinking, or not. They are creating alignment, or confusion. They are bringing people together, or driving them apart. These conversations matter, or they may not. David Isaacs says, "A primary role of leaders is to design, convene, and host conversations that matter." Developing the foundational skill of communicating effectively is a step toward fulfilling that role.

Business, like relationships, moves forward through conversations. We have many conversations every day as leaders, but how many of them matter? How do we ensure that they matter? One way a conversation matters is when it helps us push past our limits and drive business forward in a positive way. Another way is when it helps us develop the capacity of an individual or team to make a positive contribution toward efforts to drive business forward. It is our responsibility as leaders to communicate effectively with others so we achieve both of these objectives.

If we communicate effectively, we design both verbal and written conversations to result in the best possible encounter. We will "meet" well. It is important to think carefully about what we wish to communicate, to whom, and in what mode. Being clear about our objectives is critical. It means knowing what success looks like during and at the end of the conversation. Clarity about our objectives enables us to think about whom we want to communicate with, and in what manner. It means knowing which medium to use, and what style to adopt as convener and host of the conversation. Keep in mind, however, that we are not always the host. Even so, we can still design how we want to show up, what experience we want, and what results we seek.

For a conversation to matter, it must be well designed. When we convene conversations, we become responsible for creating and maintaining the environment that enables success. Regardless of the medium you use, it's important to establish rapport. Rapport is the connection that exists when people sense we are concerned enough to be fully present in the conversation. We must feel fully to connect well.

Everyone has experienced or heard stories of horrible meetings. Meetings are conversations. An awful meeting is typically the result of poorly designed and ill-convened conversations. Many meetings are only strings of monologues punctuated with bits of information that could have been shared in different ways. Most meetings do not matter in that the conversations fail to move business forward or help those present to learn and develop.

A well-convened meeting has clear objectives. People know what the purpose of the meeting is and what role they play. A well-convened meeting includes time spent enabling participants to connect with each other. It encourages people to think carefully and feel fully while the conversation occurs.

Usual and ordinary leaders call meetings without designing them well. They do not consider how best to convene their business conversations. As such, they do not make the best hosts. You are the host when you call a meeting in the same way that you're a host when you invite someone to a party. As host, you are responsible for the invitation, the experience, and the result. The same holds true when you invite someone to a conversation. Good conversation means paying close attention to the process of the conversation. If it's a conversation among multiple people, a good host hones in on the process more than the content. The host facilitates participation and ensures that each person's contribution is respected and valued according to its merits.

Designing, convening, and hosting conversations that matter is a sign that we are thinking carefully in order to communicate effectively. When we do not take the time to design what and how we communicate, it has a cascading effect that can negatively impact our teams—and our organization suffers. Why? Actions speak louder than words. To drive business forward, and to grow our capacity to develop business successfully, we need to pay attention to what we do and in what manner.

Everything we say or do as leaders communicates something. "Do as I say, not as I do" does not work with children, so we should not expect it to work with peers and employees. How we communicate gives tacit permission to those around us to use the same method and style in their work.

This is a broad analysis of communication, but it is so crucial to our development as ultra leaders. To understand, as a starting point, that communicating effectively goes a long way in leadership helps keep us intentional as we design and convene our business conversations.

All conversations should be designed with a single aim: enable high engagement to maximize positive impact. Before and during every conversation, consider how best to keep the other person engaged. Be mindful of what success looks like as a result of the conversation as well as the experience the participants in the conversation are having. This attention to design minimizes the likelihood that what we are saying and how we are saying it might create a barrier to engagement. A verbal or nonverbal miscommunication can have a serious, unintentionally negative impact.

Without focused attention and intention, many times we say or do something that creates a barrier between an individual or team's ability to engage and make the contribution we want. Remember, it is our responsibility as leaders to create the conditions that enable people to give their best voluntarily. How we communicate and design our conversations can have a positive or negative impact on how people engage and contribute.

Being mindful of the impact of our communication can carry us a long way. It invites a new and more intentional approach to what we hope to accomplish and what we experience along the way. This more intentional way of leadership seeks to influence more than coerce. In some ways, this mind-set is akin to the highest value of medicine: Do no harm.

As leaders, we can underestimate the impact our words and actions have on the people around us. At our peril, we continue to underestimate the power of our communications and their potential to trigger a counterproductive reaction in another person. We must pay more attention to what we communicate and how.

Imagine if, before we communicated anything, we became clear about what we hoped to achieve, and how we wanted the experience to be for others. This attention to design increases the probability that our communication at best enables high engagement and maximizes positive impact, and at worst does no harm.

As leaders, we take on new responsibility when we accept that conversation is a core business process and that everything we communicate has an impact. Accepting this responsibility means communicating in such a way that others stay in the game and on the field. When we are in the field, we encourage continuous forward motion for our organization and the people in it. When we communicate from this place of awareness and intention, we are not stuck in unproductive roles. We are not victims or villains, winners or losers, good guys or bad guys. We are simply seeking to communicate a message in a way that enables engagement and the positive transformation of the business, the team, and the individual.

Leading and communicating at this level requires ongoing practice. It requires continual self-reflection and discovery to become aware of the gap between our intention and the perception of others regarding what and how we communicate. Self-awareness helps us stay in the field, communicating in a way that keeps people giving their very best. Axel Clauberg, Vice President at Deutsche Telekom AG, has it right when he says, "Communication needs to be authentic and honest."

In his book *Theory U*, Otto Scharmer suggests that, just as there are levels to our thinking, there are levels to how we converse and listen to each other. If we are to communicate effectively, we must grow our capacity to listen and converse in order to engage others and lead more impactful change.

According to Scharmer, we listen in four different ways. He calls the first way "downloading." We download when we listen to confirm what we already know. This is the most superficial level of listening. In fact, it is not really listening at all; it is pausing while someone else speaks. The second way we listen is what Scharmer calls "factual listening." This occurs when we listen to become aware of new information or data that challenges our preconceived notions about a subject. Third is "empathic listening." Empathic listening happens when we listen so as to understand a situation or topic through the perspective of others. This level of listening can result in a perpetual shift, a new point of view, and a stronger emotional connection with another person. The fourth way of listening is what Scharmer calls "generative listening." This happens when we listen in order to discover what is emerging within us personally and between ourselves and other people. When we practice generative listening, we exist in the same field as the person with whom we are communicating, and we are truly working together to communicate effectively. Generative listening enables what Martin Heidegger called the "threshold occasion," which is a moment of *ec-stasis*, when something changes from one state of being to another.

Empathic and generative listening requires active and complete engagement. We must be fully present and observant. It is nonjudgmental and unconditionally constructive. When we engage in empathic and generative listening, we listen in order to connect to and learn from another person. When we learn to listen at these deeper levels, we hear the clues we need to ask someone the right question in the right way at the right moment and secure their engagement or discover a way forward that means real positive transformation.

How can we lead if we do not listen actively? If we choose to be present and observant, we are deciding to listen actively. The Chinese character for listening is comprised of several different characters. Each character represents an essential element of listening. It includes the character for you, as a person; a character for eyes, for undivided attention; a character for the heart; and one for the ears. The character for a king is also present. This suggests that, when we listen, the ear is most important. In other words, when we listen, the ear is king. David Messenger told me, "The practice of listening is one of the most underused skills in leadership. Making sure that it is front-loaded as part of our problem-solving and decision-making process is critical."

In addition to describing the four ways of listening, Scharmer explains the four ways we converse. The first way, just as with listening, is to download. We download when we speak from a "this is what they want to hear" perspective. This is the "talking nice" habit prevalent within many of our organizations. It is a superficial way of communicating, and it usually becomes a major hindrance to organizational effectiveness and success. Our tendency to download when listening and conversing is a huge factor in the perpetuation of the usual and ordinary in our organizations.

The second way we converse is to debate. We debate when we speak from a "this is what I think" perspective. Usually, when conversing at this level, we have little desire or will to change our position. This is "talking tough." What may pass for brainstorming or creative thinking in our organizations is more likely a debate of competing ideas; usually the person with the loudest or most forceful voice wins.

The third way we converse is by engaging in dialogue. We dialogue when we speak from a "seeing myself from the whole" perspective. Dialogue requires empathic listening. We must be conscious, connected, and concerned. We must practice careful thinking and feeling fully. Genuine dialogue is a process of mutual reflective inquiry.

The deepest and fourth form of conversing is called generating. Generating occurs when we focus our attention on what is moving through the conversation. There is a generative flow to the conversation. A generative conversation has the power to change the situation and participants.

One thing I stress to my clients is that it is better to use inquiry before advocacy in conversations. If we want our conversations to move beyond downloading and debating, so we can engage in real dialogue that fosters connection, the starting point is inquiry. As soon as we advocate a position, people invariably and instantaneously form an opinion and vote on whether they agree or disagree. But when we inquire, we invite deeper reflection and further dialogue.

The intention and ability to ask powerful questions is a sign that we are communicating effectively. Questioning becomes powerful when it provides others keys that unlock doors to their own self-reflection, their own personal and professional growth, or their own capacity for creativity and innovation. Powerful questions invite exploration. They evoke discovery and stimulate conversations to move past downloading and debate and into deeper examination and reflection. When we use inquiry, we demonstrate a curiosity that not only engages others but also opens the door for greater creativity and potential innovation.

Effective communication is a sign of a leader's ability to think carefully and feel fully. Janet Widmann told me, "Before I go into any conversation I make sure I'm clear on my intention for having that conversation. Is it to understand? Is it to get more information? Is it to try and influence with my point of view?" This is a strategic approach to communicating. It asks, "What is the optimal way to communicate a well-thought-out message?" By communicating this way, we facilitate a process whereby others think more carefully and feel more fully. In today's marketplace, this is a critical step. Competitive advantage is not necessarily determined by an ability to produce more for less. Competitive advantage begins with being able to outthink the competition. We are more likely to do so when we communicate effectively.

Research indicates that how teams think together best determines their performance. To think together, we must be emotionally intelligent and capable of communicating effectively. It takes leadership to enable such a dynamic environment to take shape. By communicating in a way that brings forth intelligent, informed, and purposeful action, our teams and organizations begin to move beyond business as usual.

Consider the following statements about communicating effectively. Are they true for you?

- I consider what others need to know when designing how I communicate.
- I am naturally curious about other people's perspectives and opinions.
- I convey information clearly and concisely.
- I respond to requests for my time, energy, or input promptly.
- I actively listen, giving my full attention when others are speaking.
- I am adept at making presentations to a group.
- I can clearly and enthusiastically enroll others to work with me, to realize a vision.
- I encourage dialogue by asking questions with a nonjudgmental attitude.

The ability to access the vast catalog of leadership competencies rests upon the capacity to think carefully, feel fully, and communicate effectively. Growing these three foundational skills is a must for aspiring ultra leaders. When we develop these skills, it becomes easier to put in the long miles of driving change and taking care of the people we lead.

As we grow our ability to think carefully, we get better at examining opportunities and challenges from a broader perspective. We strengthen our ability to understand the potential impact different actions have on others. We seek out and select the optimal rather than obvious solutions.

As we grow our ability to feel fully, we become more self-aware and adept at managing our emotions. We become attuned to our social environment and more capable of maintaining key relationships.

In turn, working to communicate more effectively will help us connect better with others and be more strategic, concise, and clear as we move beyond usual and ordinary and begin to lead real change.

CHAPTER SEVEN

Aim, Align, Act (A³)

I HOPE by now that my position on leadership is clear: If we are going to improve how we engage people and drive change, we must shift how we view and practice leadership. Making this shift is not easy, but it is critical. Ultimately, we can only truly change ourselves, and developing new leadership habits can be difficult for all of the reasons we have outlined thus far. That's why the ultra leadership framework includes a tool kit for those looking to push beyond usual and ordinary.

It is one thing to talk about leadership and quite another to put those principles into practice. Only by taking the step from theory to practice will we awaken ourselves and engage others to enable their maximum contribution and drive positive disruption in our organizations.

The A³ model is the capstone of the ultra leadership framework. If driven by the will to push the limits and a desire to lead, the ultra leader strives to become more conscious, connected, and concerned. The ultra leader consciously works to develop her capacity to think carefully, feel fully, and communicate effectively. A³ is the mental model and tool that helps leaders leverage those skills to engage others and drive change while simultaneously strengthening those very same skills and reinforcing the ultra leadership mind-set.

Our organizations operate in a complex and fast-paced world. A³ is intentionally designed using a simple, easy-to-recall, fast-to-use structure that meets the demands of leaders working in this environment. In our work with leaders and teams inside organizations of all sizes, we've seen a need for a tool that can function as an individual mental model as well as a social technology, supporting a shift to a new approach to leadership that moves our organizations beyond usual and ordinary. A³ provides a common language and framework that enables the ultra leadership mind-set and skill set to take root, replicate, and scale.

One leader we worked with made a compelling case for using the A³ model. "I remember one organization where 'ready, fire, aim' was the norm. Three months into my tenure, I was asked why we were not reducing head count faster. Three months after that, the same person asked me why we were not hiring faster. The level of reactivity was staggering. My approach with my team was to breathe and say, 'Before we go into reaction mode on this, let's think through the consequences so we might make some informed decisions.' I think good decision-making is about creating the breathing room to do that."

Our work has always focused on helping leaders and teams fight the tendency of the reactive "ready, fire, aim" approach—to allow breathing room, so they can aim *before* they fire. I devised the A³ model—aim, align, act—as a simple mental model and social technology to enable and develop the ultra leadership mind-set and skill set.

AIM

The pace of our work, in addition to a penchant for efficiency and expediency, can work against us. We go so fast that we forget to pay attention. It is amazing how frequently many of us stop paying attention to what is happening around us and inside us. It's for this reason that A³ begins with "aim." When we aim, we make the choice to be present and observant.

Every initiative starts with a definition of the target. When we aim, we begin a process of inquiry to grow our understanding of the target. To think carefully and strategically, we need to see beyond the present and pay attention to where we would like to go. The first target we aim at involves an inquiry around the question "Where are we going?" Asking this question presses us to stop for a moment and contemplate how we define success. Of course, our answers aren't set in stone, but they will support moving to the next step: aligning around the optimal strategy to achieve the future state we've envisioned.

Another question to ask when we aim is "Where are we now?" Careful examination of the current situation allows us to test our assumptions about why we are where we are. It is at this step—when we still haven't moved to take action—that we use the inquiry process to move our thinking and our dialogue to a deeper level.

To lead change, we have to be *consciously phenomenological*, which is a fancy way of saying "intensely curious about the realities and reasons behind any current situation." Curiosity means setting aside our preconceived notions about the current situation (which are based on our past experience) and allowing the present and future possibilities to inform us. To do this, we must develop our emotional intelligence and resilience. In essence, we need to develop our capacity to feel fully.

If it is our tendency to download, to reach for the expedient and settle for the obvious, then pausing to allow an inner dialogue or conversation with others to develop so we intentionally aim at our target may be a first step toward becoming more reflective and less impulsive and thereby more present and observant as leaders. Having identified point A, where we are now, and point B, where we want to be, we are ready to take the next step.

ALIGN

Ultra leaders choose to be creative and innovative. To drive real change, we must imagine a different future just beyond the threshold. That requires careful thinking that, as Brian Arthur explains, "allows inner knowing to emerge" and invites creativity and innovation into our processes, thereby aligning them around the optimal strategy for hitting what we're aiming at. Through careful thinking, we encourage creativity and make space for innovation. We create an opportunity for something or someone to move from one state of being to another.

The trap of the "ready, fire, aim" approach means we

make decisions based solely on the past: past information, past decisions, and past experiences. By taking the time to align, we engage our imaginations and consider all options. We study the advantages, disadvantages, and implications of each course of option under consideration. The intentional curiosity we exhibit when we align is what allows for multiple possibilities to emerge so we can discover the optimal solutions and not just the obvious ones. By reflecting before jumping into action, we not only open the door to more opportunities, but we also reduce the likelihood of costly missteps as we move to execute our plans with greater alignment.

The important questions we ask when we align include these: "What are our options to get where we want to go?" "Which route is best?" "How will we work together?" Exploring these questions allows the future to factor into our decision-making. This step of our thinking and conversing is where the past and future intersect. In the parlance of Brian Arthur, we are "allowing inner knowing to emerge." It is where we want to take our strategic thinking if we are serious about leading change and hope to develop innovative and creative strategies and solutions in service of that end.

It is important to note that, when used as a social technology, this second step in the A³ process is an intentionally reflective and dialogical experience of inquiry. Saying we're going to change is one thing. We need to take steps that encourage others to step up to change with us. When we invite others into an "align" conversation, we create the possibility that a threshold occasion will occur, enabling real and profound change to emerge and take hold. This is the step in the process where we intentionally deepen our thinking, listening, and conversing to encourage real dialogue and enable an experience of generativity.

As conveners and hosts of these A³ conversations, it falls on us to maintain a space for whatever possibilities emerge through our inquiry. We do this best by getting out of the way. Although this is the step that our external pressures and internal voices would have us skip, ultra leadership requires a conscious and courageous act of letting go of what we believe so as to allow for the truly innovative strategy or solution to emerge. By letting go of prior beliefs, we allow new opinions and solutions to facilitate real connection and more effective collaboration.

If external pressures and internal anxieties had their way, we would skip this "align" step entirely. We'd tell ourselves it is not an option to slow down, or that these "align" conversations are too messy and a waste of time. We tell ourselves things like: *I need to look as if I'm moving and not sitting around and thinking. We have to go fast. This is too different. It's a waste of time. It'll never work. If we do this, something terrible will happen.*

Many of us simply wish to move past this step. We may provide the solutions for our teams so we can skip this step and just keep going. This second step of the A³ process is difficult for many leaders because "align" conversations can be messy, or they can produce conflict for the very reason that they invite creativity into the strategic problem-solving and decision-making process. Creativity is messy.

It's imperative that we contain our internal anxieties to handle external pressures because we cannot skip this second step. It is vital. Skip this step and, rest assured, you will be downloading and perpetuating the usual and ordinary.

ACT

We are always moving. The question is whether or not our activity is aligned with our organizational strategy and purpose. Are we moving in the right direction? Committing time to the first two steps of A³ greatly increases the likelihood that our actions will move us in the right direction. The third step, "act," involves laying out out a strategy and making plans to act quickly, strategically, and with alignment.

These are the questions to ask as we act: "What must happen?" "What does success look like?" "Who drives what?" This third step ensures shared clarity about roles, responsibilities, accountabilities, timing, and how we measure success. Shared clarity creates a positive environment in which teams can live, work, and breathe. The right environment enables talent to engage and perform at a high level over time and with minimal interference and distraction.

Our objective at this step is to put the pieces together. Up to this point, we have moved slowly, at least more slowly than we are comfortable with, in order to go faster now and as we move to execute our plans. After aiming at our desired target and aligning on a path to our desired future state, at this step we choose the best course of action and chart it out, coordinate action, and ensure we hit our target. It is through careful attention to the "act" step of the A³ process that we manifest the ultra leadership attributes of being strategic and purposeful.

Some of us have a tendency for impulsive, knee-jerk decision-making. Others may take the opposite approach and sink into what is sometimes derisively called analysis paralysis. As a social technology for collective inquiry, the A³ model is a leveler. It slows down those who tend to be more impulsive and speeds up those who may become stuck in analysis paralysis. When we apply the A³ tool kit, we shift from an impulsive or "analysis paralysis" approach to one that employs deeper thinking, generative dialogue, and purposeful action. How we use A³ depends on the needs of the situation. We can use A³ individually or collaboratively. Everyone can remember "aim, align, act," which makes it an easily replicable process for teams and organizations.

To review, here are some of the most fundamental questions the A³ model reminds us to ask.

AIM:

- Where are we going?
- Where are we now?

ALIGN:

- What are our options to get where we want to go?
- Which route is best? (Check assumptions. Prioritize based on the implications of each potential course of action.)
- How will we work together? (Think shared experience and the rules of engagement.)

ACT:

- What must happen? (Think milestones and tasks.)
- What does success look like? (Think outcomes, timing, and metrics.)

- Who drives what? (Think ownership, accountability, and roles and responsibilities.)

If you are using A³ to coach another person or group of individuals, you might ask more questions. To help the person or group be present and observant, and *aim* well, you would ask:

- What is your situation?
- What is the best possible outcome?
- What's in the way?
- How are you contributing to the status quo?
- What absolutely *must* happen?

To help spark creativity and encourage innovative thinking to *align*, you might ask:

- What questions are you considering?
- What options come to mind?
- How does each option get you closer to your best possible outcome?
- What might you have to let go of or learn in order to achieve your best possible outcome?

Questions that aid the person or group to *act* with more strategic and purposeful intent include these:

- What will you do?
- What's the simplest and best next step?
- Whom do you need to or want to engage for support?

I presented questions for reflection at the conclusions of each chapter. These questions are meant to aid you as you take your first steps on the path toward ultra leadership. They help you aim at your starting point. How strong is your drive to lead? How conscious, connected, and concerned do you think you are? How careful is your thinking? How fully do you feel? Are you communicating effectively?

Some leaders use A^3 to frame their days and guide their decisions about how to spend their time, energy, and resources. Each morning they "aim" at the day ahead. Their inquiry looks like this:

- What do I want to accomplish today?
- What do I want my team to accomplish today?
- What does my team need from me today?
- How can I grow myself as a leader today?
- What does going beyond usual and ordinary look like today?
- If today were my last day, how would I want to be remembered?
- What behaviors and practices will ensure I leave this legacy?

The philosopher Ludwig Wittgenstein said, "We cannot know a thing without a word for it." Our work with A³, with leaders and teams, focuses on generating that "word." Using A³ as the framework for our collective inquiry, we build an organizational, team, or individual road map. The road map becomes a focal point we use to regularly review and evaluate our progress, examine any changes to the situation, and ensure alignment with individual and organizational vision and purpose. We conceived the road map as a simple visual tool for leaders and teams to use to create alignment and coordinate action.

When we build a road map with a team, we use the A³ process to guide the conversation. We aim at where they want to go and where they are in the moment. We ask about their business objectives and their objectives for working together as a team. We ask about the current state of the team. How aligned are they around existing vision, strategy, and roles and responsibilities? How would they assess their current individual and team capacity? How well coordinated are the actions they take?

With a better sense of point A and agreement on point B, we can populate the column in the road map with the ideal outcomes. This column represents their point B—the future state the team will strive to create. Some teams attach such metrics as specific revenue, engagement, or customer-satisfaction targets to their ideal outcomes.

When we have ideal outcomes identified, we shift to an "align" conversation. We explore what it will take to achieve their results and the possible courses of action. As the team considers options, they discuss how each option gets them closer to their best possible outcome. We ask them to explore what they might have to let go of or learn in order to achieve their ideal outcomes. We explore what they might have to do in order to create more alignment, build their individual and collective capacity, and better coordinate their actions in order to achieve success.

Having explored multiple options for moving the business forward and creating the conditions necessary for them to engage and contribute more fully, we shift the conversation and act to identify milestones that populate a work stream on the road map. These milestones represent what needs to be done to achieve a particular outcome. Each ideal outcome has its own work stream and milestones, so it is clear what needs to be done and by whom. The road map is becoming clear by this point, but the team still needs to discuss the plan to move forward. It's great to have milestones on a road map, but how do they become actual significant accomplishments? The team considers the best next step for each work stream. They identify who

Team Roadmap

Workstream	MILESTONE 1	MILESTONE 2	MILESTONE 3	MILESTONE 4	MILESTONE 5	MILESTONE 6
1						
2						
3						
4						
5						

Vision Statement goes here.

SCORECARD
(Success Measures)

Outcomes	Metrics

on the team is going to own a particular work stream—the individual who is accountable when the team leader asks if the team is moving forward in the right direction.

By the time we finish, we have a robust road map outlining our vision, outcomes, and strategy. The process of talking through the road map, when we act to put the pieces together, brings us very close to where we need to be regarding strategic decisions. The road map helps a team decide how to allocate time, energy, and resources to achieve their ideal outcomes.

The road map becomes a regular discussion point for the team moving forward. It keeps them thinking carefully and communicating effectively. Once a month the team has a fast, ninety-minute meeting at which they review the road map and assess progress and challenges. Those meetings are also designed and convened using the A^3 process. Teams aim at where they are on the path, what is working, where they are stuck. When something does get in the way of a team achieving its goals, they have an "align" conversation to explore how to act to take the best next step.

We use the road map process with different types of businesses over various lengths of time. In one example, we worked with a large organization that honed their strategy over many years. In another, we helped a small team identify what was preventing them from reaching their goals and also how to pave a new path forward. We use the road map process with individuals as well.

In fact, the road map process provides a strong point of confluence between the work of the team and individual contributions to that work. If we complete a road map with a team, a member of that team can also create his or her own road map that focuses on a particular work stream. If a team member's primary role is to improve customer satisfaction, he can create an individual-contribution road map that lets him think of things ahead of time. He then shares the information with the team, thereby alerting them to what he plans on contributing to the overall business objective. He can also share what he plans to contribute to the shared experience of the team and to his own development. We've found that this approach keeps team members engaged. It illustrates what a person needs to contribute to a team over time and therefore ensures engagement.

We use road maps when we work with individual leaders in coaching situations, too. We aim to get a clear picture of their current reality and identify business and leadership development objectives. We align on a course of action that gets the leader practicing with new styles and tools to help him achieve more as he acts to go beyond usual and ordinary to engage his teams and move things forward.

A VIRTUOUS CYCLE

Using the A³ model puts us on a path of continuous, multi-dimensional development. It's a simple tool that provides a common language and process that, over time, creates more "conscious competence." Every time we intentionally aim, align, and act, we are becoming more conscious, connected, and concerned and are growing our capacity to think carefully, feel fully, and communicate effectively.

Existential psychologists Irvin Yalom and Rollo May, along with philosopher Martin Buber, often spoke of the infinite possibility that exists in the "in-between"—when two subjects connect with a spirit of openness. Our leadership challenge is to encounter people and situations with openness, to see what may emerge in the "in-between" of the change process. The A³ model—aim, align, act—can be a powerful tool that enables leaders to act from the intersection—the in-between—of their knowledge of the past, their vision of the future, and a deeper connection with themselves and the world around them.

When we apply A³, we challenge ourselves and encourage others to think more carefully and act with greater openness. And we remain aware of the first reality of any business, which is to create value for customers and stakeholders. A³ can take us beyond usual and ordinary to a place of newfound effectiveness and success. As leaders of change, we are breaking the "ready, fire, aim" habit and replacing it with aim, align, and act. We grow our capacity to create stronger alignment, build capacity in those around us, and coordinate action to inspire higher engagement and move things forward to drive real change. It all begins with an intention to go beyond usual and ordinary and to aim before we fire. When that happens, the possibilities become endless.

Developing our capacity to lead is a lifelong journey and daily practice. It is a courageous act to accept the call to push past our limits and lead in a new way. Every step of A³ supports that courageous intention. At the "aim" step, we are called to look carefully and unflinchingly at our current reality and explore what we most want for the future. It takes courage to be fully present and observant. At the "align" step, we are called to be creative and innovative. It takes courage to open up this messy, sometimes inconvenient process of collaboration and inquiry. It takes courage to invite dialogue rather than debate. It takes courage to let go of our preconceived notions and outcomes. And it takes courage to face the real and unrelenting pressure always to go faster and do more with a determination to be more careful and deliberate in how we think, listen, and converse. At the "act" step, we are called to be strategic and purposeful. It takes courage to do things differently in order to lead change. It takes courage to meet resistance with curiosity and compassion. It takes courage to follow up and follow through.

Theodore Roosevelt said:

> *The credit belongs to the man who is actually in the arena; whose face is marred by dust and sweat and blood. Who strives valiantly, who errs; who comes up short again and again, because there is no effort without error and shortcoming. But who does actually strive to do the deeds; who knows great enthusiasms and great devotions; who spends himself in a worthy cause. Who at the best knows, in the end, the triumph of high achievement, and who at the worst, if he fails, at least, he fails while daring greatly, so that his place shall never be with those cold and timid souls who neither know victory nor defeat.*

I have been privileged to work with and coach many leaders who inspire me with their courage to go to the edge and lead. They are "in the arena." In chapter 8, I will share the story of one of these ultra leaders. His story represents what it means to go beyond usual and ordinary. He faced all the challenges we have discussed in this book, and he chose to step into each one. He is a lifelong learner who understands that leadership is a lifelong journey.

CHAPTER EIGHT

Ultra Leadership in Action

STRONG LEADERS do not lament change. They do not embrace the status quo. They do not try to tweak the "machine" so it runs just right; rather, they try to keep themselves, their people, and their organizations healthy and growing. They're continuously pushing the limits to cause positive disruption. They're continuously working to get people to willingly, enthusiastically, and repeatedly say yes and engage and contribute to purposeful change. They have a drive to shake things up and an ability to feel fully, think carefully, and communicate effectively in order to make that happen.

The work of change leadership is like a challenging sea voyage. To be competitive, we must go to the edge, push farther, and adjust, over and over again. This is particularly true in times of organizational change. Many factors contribute to successful organizational change. *How* we lead and implement change affects how people engage and contribute. Some boats and ships are more seaworthy than others, and some organizations are more change-worthy than others.

Todd Burger is President and CEO at AAA MountainWest. When Todd arrived, AAA MountainWest was stuck. For seven years, membership rates and revenue had showed little to no growth. Clearly, something had to change. I have known Todd for a number of years, and I can say unequivocally that he embodies ultra leadership. In his new role as President he was determined to shake things up and tap into the enormous market potential and grow his new organization. As a native Montanan and longtime AAA leader, Todd was committed to lead change in his organization from a place of consciousness, connection, and concern for his employees and AAA Mountain-West's members.

Over the course of our working together, Todd has grown quite familiar with the A³ model. To lead change of the magnitude he was envisioning, Todd committed to modeling the behaviors and practices that he expected his leaders to adopt. Our coaching focused on how Todd could best lead by example as he set out to make his organization more change-worthy.

We had three objectives. To bring about the change that would stimulate real and sustained growth, he would have to create alignment, build bench strength, and coordinate action in a very different way than the organization had become accustomed to. We crafted a change leadership strategy to aid him in that work.

READY, AIM, LEAD

Like many of us, Todd likes to go fast, so he had to be very intentional in the early days to slow down and aim well before jumping to action. Our initial work centered on helping Todd be present and observant as he established relationships within his new organization. He aspired to learn from his board, senior leadership team, and employees. His curiosity piqued theirs. People soon wanted to see a preview of what was to come, which allowed Todd to share his vision and enroll people as partners in building a strategy to grow the organization. Through his many conversations, he was able to evaluate the change-worthiness of his organization.

That initial period of intentional curiosity, of consciously connecting and listening, produced many conversations that matter. In the process, his stakeholders began to align around his vision and accept his call to partner with him in leading the organization through an exciting time of change and improvement. What's more, because Todd was overtly inviting people into what he called "aim" conversations, his leaders began to experience and learn the benefits of using the A^3 model. The conversations were themselves beginning a learning and development process for his leaders.

THE ABCS OF CHANGE LEADERSHIP

Wanting change and being able to change are two different things. In an environment of significant change, we can only make our organizations change-worthy by ensuring that we are prepared to lead. My colleague and exceptional executive coach, Pat Newmann, and I devised a "Change Leader's Checklist" to help leaders and teams gauge and develop their change-worthiness. The checklist lays out the ABCs of change leadership: alignment, bench strength, and coordinated action. (The "Change Leader's Checklist" is available for free on our website. Visit www.GiulianoAssociates.com to get your copy.)

ALIGNMENT

At the outset of this book, I stated that change efforts are unsuccessful because of a leadership deficiency.

Successful change requires an executive sponsor who has the will and skill to build a coalition for change. At MountainWest, Todd Burger was that sponsor. Early in his tenure, he gathered his leaders to co-create a clear direction forward—a vision, mission, and strategy for the organization and for the change that lay ahead. The team worked to build a plan that tackled structural adjustments, roles and responsibilities, and systems and processes needed to achieve their objectives. They aligned around key milestones and timelines, and everyone understood how success would be measured.

Everything was captured in the organizational road map that the team co-owned with Todd's support. Todd and his leadership team, working together in this way, grew their capacity to connect with one another and work across functions to collaborate. Creating the road map together illustrated how interdependent they were. This insight enabled them to see the organization more systemically and to see how their work intertwined. The road map process created a level of shared clarity that led to coordinated action.

BENCH STRENGTH

Included in the organizational strategy for change was a plan to engage employees throughout the process so they could continue to learn and grow as they took part in making the change work. Engaging the senior leadership team to co-create alignment established a business context in which we could simultaneously begin to build individual and collective leadership capacity, increasing organizational bench strength.

While Todd was familiar with A³ and the other tools in our ultra leadership tool kit, his team was not. We worked to introduce a common language of leadership and encourage the adoption of the A³ model, as well as a number of additional leadership tools that would enable a consistent approach to leadership and a cascade of that approach to all people managers and employees. Through their diligence in developing themselves, the leadership team has built the bench strength of the organization. Now, when a new problem, challenge, or opportunity arises, it is not uncommon for someone to say, "We need to have an 'aim' conversation."

It takes focused attention and intention for leaders at every level to shift an organization's culture toward change-worthiness. One of the goals during times of change is to keep people engaged even when unavoidable business disruptions occur. The common leadership framework, language, and tool kit applied by Todd and his team helped to do just that.

MountainWest leaders use the organizational road map as a mechanism for coordinating action, reviewing it monthly, and revising it as needed to guide strategic activities through each year. Regular review facilitates ongoing follow-up and follow-through. With tracking and adjustment tools in place, Todd and his team can manage and coordinate action, so more is done in less time and with less effort. They committed to a RACI model to identify roles and responsibilities and encourage greater accountability. One of the things that they've noticed as a result of taking these steps is that it has made them a very nimble organization. The alignment they maintain enables them to go faster.

Their efforts to create shared clarity and build organizational capacity let them take a radical step forward in how they engage people and evaluate performance. Todd and his team decided that one tangible sign of their change would be to fundamentally change their performance-management system. They ended their annual performance-appraisal process and replaced it with a quarterly "A³ Performance" conversation between a manager and each employee. These conversations shifted the focus from a review of past performance to a forward-looking coaching and feedback conversation in which a manager and an employee identify and agree on future contributions and development activities that will support those contributions. All managers received training and coaching on how to engage their team members from the new perspective.

The A³ Performance process is designed to ensure alignment to the organizational vision and strategy, build bench strength by facilitating ongoing learning and development, and reinforce the leadership framework and skill set and coordinating action by linking individual contributions back to the organizational road map. The output of these A³ Performance conversations is a personal A³ Performance road map, in which each employee identifies and commits to contributing to the business, their team's shared experience, and their own ongoing development.

During the A³ Performance conversation, an employee highlights three to four contributions she will make to the business in the upcoming quarter. Her personal road map also includes two to three contributions she commits to making to her team to ensure a positive shared experience.

One example of a commitment an employee might make to the team is to make clearer requests of his manager. Or, perhaps, he will commit to seek feedback, or ask for help if he is feeling overwhelmed.

Populating a personal A³ Performance roadmap also forces employees to think carefully about what they will contribute to their development. Do they want to receive technical training? Do they want to read more on a particular topic? Do they want to run a 5K?

These quarterly conversations between each people manager and employee help create alignment, build bench strength, and coordinate action. They help redefine the relationship between manager and employee. They require leaders to engage more consciously, and they facilitate careful thinking. Every person, including Todd, prints and posts his personal A³ Performance roadmap in his office or at his desk, which promotes greater accountability.

The commitment of Todd and his leadership team to go beyond usual and ordinary has yielded positive results. After multiple years of little to no growth, the organization, in just the last few years, has seen positive growth in every key metric including membership, revenue, and sales of key products and services. They know they're on a journey. They have a long way to go and face stiff competition in a rapidly changing marketplace. However, they've taken the steps necessary to build a change-worthy organization that can weather the seas of change that are always on the horizon.

Transformation inside an organization takes time; the period between the beginning and seeing tangible results can be long. Many times it requires a timeframe of twelve, twenty-four, or thirty-six months. Change management inside an organization typically focuses on structure; maybe it entails reorganizing a department, or introducing a new IT system or software. But the reason change efforts often fail is because the new systems are put into place and left on their own. We hope something great will happen as a result of the change, but do little to ensure that it does. The change leadership approach, the one that an ultra leadership approach enables, is much broader, in that we are not trying just to change a structure or system; we are working to change a culture and grow a new leadership mind-set and skill set to drive the desired change.

Changing a culture begins with changing how we see leadership. It means changing how we as leaders show up every day to talk and listen to our teams. In the end, each person reacts to change in his or her own way. A manager could tell me that my organization is changing, and the way I react is going to be different than the way someone else does. We each may receive the message in a different way and respond to it in a different way. Change leadership takes that into account; it anticipates it by implementing a systematic approach built upon the ultra leadership framework and using the "Change Leader's Checklist" to focus efforts.

Our work with Todd Burger and AAA MountainWest centered on a change leadership approach, but different systems and processes also needed to change to support a new style of leadership. It was a significant change to pivot from performance reviews to contribution management. The shared message that supported the effort was this: "We are on a journey. We are changing our culture; this is how we want to show up and work together; this is what we are working toward."

Under Todd Burger's leadership, AAA MountainWest set a new course and reimagined its leadership approach, became more change-worthy, and, as a result, is on its way to a more viable future. The cost of not changing could result in losing competitive advantage and market share. For some organizations, that means disappearing. Many organizations that have failed at change no longer exist. An organization dies when it arrives at the point in its life cycle when it must change to survive but does not. Smart leaders look at what is happening in the economy and marketplace and ask the hard question: Are we still creating the kind of value that we must to attract customers? Undertaking a major change initiative means recognizing that we need to change how we do business, or change what we provide, in order to survive. Succeeding requires ultra leadership that pushes the limits and engages others to join together in the important work of driving real change.

Conclusion

AT THE OUTSET of this book, I noted that we face challenges in our organizations that only a new paradigm of leadership can solve. We are failing to drive change successfully, and our people are simply not engaged. According to Gallup, the economic cost of low engagement alone is between $450 billion and $550 billion annually. I introduced the ultra leadership framework and A³ tool kit that has helped leaders go beyond usual and ordinary, engage people, and lead real change.

Keeping people engaged and contributing as part of a high-performing team is hard work. It requires focused intention and regular attention. It is our responsibility to create shared clarity that sustains alignment. It is our responsibility to keep bench strength high and to be always building individual and team capacity. It is our responsibility to coordinate action to ensure smart and fast execution and delivery.

There's a phrase that many in business have been using for some time now. Typically it's a manager in a leadership role telling someone else that they need to "move the needle." That is, they need to cause some change; they need to increase revenue or reduce the cost associated with increasing said revenue. There is a call to action: "Let's get something done." The problem is that that call and the subsequent action tend to be usual and ordinary.

I understand the manager's motivation. Demands for our time and attention continue to rise. We get evaluated on whether or not we move the needle. We fall into a habit of reaching for the obvious and most expedient solution so we can keep up as best we can. But this pattern represents the usual and ordinary and only gets us more of the same—low engagement, failed change efforts, and lackluster performance.

The results of a study conducted by researchers Nicholas Bloom, Raffaella Sadun, and John Van Reenen were summarized recently in the *Harvard Business Review*. The results found:

> *Many organizations throughout the world are very badly managed. Well-run companies set stretch targets on productivity and other parameters, base the compensation and promotions they offer on meeting those targets, and*

constantly measure results—but many firms do none of those things. Second, our indicators of better management and superior performance are strongly correlated with measures such as productivity, return on capital employed, and firm survival. Third, management makes a difference in shaping national performance. Our analysis shows, for example, that variation in management accounts for nearly a quarter of the roughly 30% productivity gap between the U.S. and Europe.

The team at Prana Business conducted some research of S&P 500 companies and found that in 1975 only 17 percent of an organization's value was due to intangible assets. By 2014, intangible assets account for over 80 percent of an organization's value. Included among an organization's intangible assets are its human capital (people) and its ability to execute well. The impact of leadership on how well or how poorly these intangible assets are nurtured and developed cannot be overstated. To say that leadership is the key determinant of success in today's business world is truer now than it ever was.

Given the challenges we face in our organizations today, the statistics illustrating our shortcomings around employee engagement and driving change, and the make-or-break role of leadership, I want to issue a new call to action. Yes, let's move the needle. But let's use a new approach. I hope you'll consider accepting the call and make these commitments:

I commit to going beyond usual and ordinary.

I commit to using my personal power to engage others more than my title or position.

I commit to becoming more conscious as a leader.

I commit to a daily practice and a lifelong journey of personal and leadership development.

I commit to being fully connected to others: my team members, peers, and stakeholders.

I commit to demonstrating real concern for others by taking time and expending energy to make them feel intrinsically valuable.

I commit to thinking carefully in the face of rising demands and pressure to conform.

I commit to feeling fully—becoming more emotionally intelligent, self-aware, able to self-manage, and able to engage others.

I commit to communicating effectively—taking time to listen, use inquiry, and clearly convey strategic and personal messages.

I commit to being present and observant as I engage new people and new situations.

I commit to being creative and innovative as I consider how to drive change and enable positive transformation.

I commit to giving time and space for curiosity to enable alignment around the optimal solution and not just the obvious one.

I commit to creating alignment about where I want to go and where I am before I take a step.

I commit to the growth and development of my team to build and maintain bench strength.

I commit to coordinating action so that my time, energy, and resources are well allocated.

I commit to aiming before I fire.

I commit to align my thinking and the people around me.

I commit to acting strategically and with purpose.

I commit to getting out of my comfort zone on a regular basis.

I commit to go to the edge.

I commit to push farther.

I commit to repeat all of this every day.

Making the climb up to Hope Pass was a challenge for me. The experience was beyond usual and ordinary. Running ultra distances is still challenging. It will always be hard work. But I'm getting smarter about how I approach it. Leadership will always be hard work. It can get easier if we get smarter about how we approach it.

Stepping up to ultra leadership requires our full attention and intention. It is a daily practice and a lifelong journey. It is a journey that heroes make. It is a journey that brings about stronger, more effective, and more authentic leadership. This book is offered as support for those who would answer the call and commit to this practice and journey.

We need ultra leaders who answer the call to become more conscious, connected, and concerned and more skillful at thinking, feeling, and communicating in order to engage others and drive real change.

Will you answer the call?

We have three choices: Turn back. Stand still. Or step forward. To go to the edge and push farther, over and over again, takes courage.

In the words of Friedrich Nietzsche: "Have ye courage, O my brethren?... Not the courage before witnesses, but anchorite and eagle courage, which not even a God any longer beholdeth?... He hath heart who knoweth fear but vanquisheth it; who seeth the abyss, but with pride. He who seeth the abyss but with eagle's eyes, he who with eagle's talons graspeth the abyss: he hath courage."

See you on the trail.

Additional Resources

THE ULTRA LEADERSHIP CHECKLIST AND 360

The Ultra Leadership Checklist and 360 is a comprehensive assessment tool for leaders that measures three skills critical for success, as well as a leader's foundational drive to lead. The Ultra Leadership Checklist and 360 provides leaders with a solid assessment of their strength in these four areas and also helps leaders identify what learning opportunities exist to grow their capacity to push the limits and inspire high engagement and maximize the contributions of others. Visit www.UltraLeadership.com to access the Ultra Leadership Checklist and 360.

THE "CHANGE LEADER'S CHECKLIST"

The "Change Leader's Checklist" is an assessment tool for leaders that examines an organization's readiness to lead change successfully by laying out the many factors and variables that deserve consideration and attention. The "Change Leader's Checklist" is organized into three categories that illustrate the ABCs of Change Leadership:

A is for *Alignment*: Create, with leaders, a clear direction (vision, mission, strategy) and a plan (structure, roles and responsibilities, systems and processes) to achieve it.

B is for *Bench Strength*: Build leadership and organizational capacity and culture to a state of change-worthiness.

C is for *Coordinated Action*: Ensure ongoing follow-up and follow-through with tracking and adjustment mechanisms to lead and manage through the change.

Visit www.GiulianoAssociates.com to download your free copy of the "Change Leader's Checklist."

About the Author

DR. GREG GIULIANO gets leaders and teams to go beyond usual and ordinary. Well-known for his ability to synthesize complex information quickly and for his fast-paced, impactful communications, Greg designs personal- and team-development strategies that create alignment and build the leadership muscle required to coordinate action and lead real change. Greg has coached senior executives and leadership teams all over the world to accelerate their development and grow their capacity to engage others and lead.

Greg heads up Giuliano Associates, a consulting firm specializing in executive coaching, team and organization development, and leadership development. Greg's personal motto, "Go to the edge. Push farther. Repeat." provides the foundation for his work: to grow "ultra leadership," which is the will to go beyond usual and ordinary and push the limits, combined with the skill to get people to willingly, enthusiastically, and repeatedly engage and contribute to important work. He is the creator of the Ultra Leadership Checklist and 360 and author of *The Hero's Journey: Toward a More Authentic Leadership* (2014).

Some of the organizations Greg has worked with include Cisco, Veritas, BMC Software, AAA, CITI, Philips, Blue Shield of California, Red Lion Hotels, Northwest Farm Credit Services, Recurrent Energy, QuickLogic, Goodwill Industries, Barbells 4 Boobs, and Oxfam GB.

Avid trail runners, Greg and his wife live in their now empty nest in Rancho Santa Margarita, California.

CONNECT WITH GREG:

www.UltraLeadership.com
www.GiulianoAssociates.com
greg@giulianoassociates.com
(844) 519-6506

www.linkedin.com/in/greggiuliano

www.ingramcontent.com/pod-product-compliance
Lightning Source LLC
Chambersburg PA
CBHW071553200326
41519CB00021BB/6726